New Worlds for the Deaf

**The story of the pioneering
Lakeside School for the Deaf
in rural Mexico**

Cataloguing in Publication

Burton, Gwen, author
    New Worlds for the Deaf: The Story of the Pioneering Lakeside School for
    the Deaf in rural Mexico
/ Gwen Chan Burton

Issued in print and electronic formats.
ISBN 978-0-9952889-8-0 (paperback).--ISBN 978-0-9952889-9-7 (ebook)

1. Mexico--Deaf Education. 2. Deaf Education--Language.
3. Deaf children--Means of communication.
4. Education of Hearing Disabled--Methods. I. Title.

ISBN 978-0-9952889-8-0
First edition 2020
Text and map © 2020 by Gwen Burton

Cover design: Trevor Burton. Teacher Lupita helps students Paty and Mario
study the globe made by the school's founders, Jackie Hartley and Roma Jones.

Sombrero Books, Box 4, Ladysmith B.C. V9G 1A1, Canada

New Worlds for the Deaf

The story of the pioneering
Lakeside School for the Deaf
in rural Mexico

GWEN CHAN BURTON

SB

SOMBRERO BOOKS, B.C., CANADA

Contents

Lake Chapala area showing location of school and students' home villages

Preface

In a small town in western Mexico a deaf child, unschooled, encountered two Canadian women concerned by his inability to communicate. Thus was born the Lakeside School for the Deaf in Jocotepec on Lake Chapala in 1979. It offered free specialized education to deaf children and youth. Over the next 15 years the school grew, flourished and acquired international recognition.

This is the story of a community—Mexican, local expatriate, and international—that was inspired by the project and determined to make a difference in the lives of deaf children, many from impoverished families.

It is the story of a school for the deaf that developed a unique home-based boarding program to cater to children from a wide rural area.

It is a work in praise of the amazing Mexican staff who accepted the challenge of teaching in a demanding specialty and whose dedication, love and skill brought language, laughter and livelihood to so many deaf students.

Included in this book are the sometimes unbelievable background stories of many of the children and youths who arrived at the school gate with no language and limited understanding of the world around them. They found friendship and community at the school and entered a new world of communication that gave them access to knowledge of the wider world.

As a Canadian teacher of the deaf, I was part of that exciting project, initially as a teacher then as the school's director, for almost eleven years. This book is based partly on my memory of those long-past years. But it relies mainly on accounts that were written at the time of the events, including detailed newsletters sent to supporters three times a year; biographies and updates supplied to sponsors of individual children; local press reports of special events; the weekly school newspaper for parents written in simple Spanish, and my own letters to fellow Canadian Susan van Gurp who taught at the school with me for the first two years. Unfortunately, although I attended the monthly meetings of the Board of Directors, I do not have copies of the minutes of most of those meetings.

The primary focus of this book is on the students' education and activities at the school. I apologize that it has not been possible to credit here all the many hard-working supporters whose names and fund-raising achievements were essential to the school's success.

Various people, including my former colleagues, have insisted that the history of the Lakeside School for the Deaf is a story worth telling. It is the story of a dream realized.

The opening chapter and the last three are written in chronological order of events; the other chapters are organized by theme—like the boarding program, teachers, fund-raising. The mini-biographies of students are grouped into three chapters, placed at intervals through the book, based on the year when the children first entered the school.

Along the way, the book offers many glimpses of the local culture and traditions, which are just as relevant today as they were in the 1980s.

Gwen Chan Burton, November 2019.

1

The early years, 1979–1982

The founders: Jackie Hartley and Roma Jones

How did it come about that two retired Canadian women started a school for the deaf in a dusty pueblo in rural Mexico, when they had no experience in teaching the deaf, only limited Spanish, no school building and no funding? Over the next 15 years, the school gained international acclaim for providing specialized education for scores of deaf children, including many from distant villages.

The education of profoundly deaf children is recognized, worldwide, as one of the most difficult and costly forms of special education. Despite this, Jackie Hartley and Roma Jones were determined to help the local deaf children and were tenacious in seeking assistance. Against the odds, their pioneering school continued to thrive, even after they themselves returned to Canada.

In the summer of 1979, Jackie and Roma, then in their late 50s, drove a camper van from Vancouver Island, British Columbia, to Mexico. Arriving in the town of Jocotepec (population 9000), on the shores of beautiful Lake Chapala, they decided to spend their retirement years there, in leisurely pursuit of their artistic interests: painting, photography, crafts and woodworking. These dreams were never realized; instead, their waking hours became entirely focused on meeting the needs of disadvantaged Mexican children.

Jackie Hartley (left) and Roma Jones

It all started when Jackie, strolling around the plaza in those early days, kept encountering a young boy with a shy smile who seemed to want to be friends. Jackie soon realized that he was deaf, had no speech and no means of communicating. Rogelio, aged 10, and his equally deaf 7-year-old sister, Aurora, had never been to school. With their parents' permission, Jackie and Roma began teaching them. Their first classroom was the camper van.

Both Jackie and Roma had some teaching experience. Jackie had taught primary school students, including many indigenous children, for several years in British Columbia before bringing up her own four children. After her pharmacist husband died, Jackie had spent six months in Europe studying art before she journeyed to Mexico.

Roma had been a teacher for a time in Jamaica with CUSO, a Canadian government organization for professionals volunteering in developing nations. Divorced, she brought up her daughter as a single mother while working as a psychiatric nurse in Vancouver and Calgary. She later completed a Fine Arts degree. A multi-talented woman, Roma once built a house herself and gave it away, for the cost of the materials, to a needy family. Before her vacation trip to Mexico with long-time friend Jackie, Roma was enjoying teaching art in schools in northern Alberta. She resigned from that position in 1979, after deciding to settle in Jocotepec.

Lyn Hallinger provided help with teaching speech

Soon after they started teaching young Rogelio and Aurora, Jackie and Roma were introduced to Lyn Hallinger, an American resident in Ajijic. Lyn had been giving speech and language classes two afternoons a week to several deaf youngsters—Veronica, Mario, Rafael and sometimes Lourdes—since the mid-1970s.

The children would struggle to recall how to voice the sounds of words they never heard. Lyn had persuaded local schools to allow them to attend regular classes in K-2, saying that, "While the children do miss a lot... they are no longer excluded from their peer group." She was not a qualified speech therapist, but had gained practical training in the US as the parent of a deaf daughter educated in the oral tradition.[1]

When the Hallingers travelled, Jane Osburn and Esther Coster—full-time residents and, later, Deaf School Board members—filled in as best they could, "to keep the children busy." Lyn was very concerned that, if and when she should leave Ajijic, the program would collapse for lack of a replacement.

Jackie and Roma travelled twice weekly to Ajijic to learn from Lyn the techniques for the difficult task of teaching deaf students to vocalize and understand spoken words. When the Hallingers moved back to the US in late 1979, two of Lyn's students—Veronica and Mario—began attending full-day classes five days a week in Jocotepec, joining students Rogelio and Aurora. As Esther Coster later wrote, "Roma and Jackie arrived on the scene in Jocotepec and started an authentic school." Jackie's initial name for the school—the Saint Francis Lyn School for the Deaf—included 'Lyn' in honour of Lyn Hallinger.

Learning to teach deaf children

Roma and Jackie had discovered that there were no schools for the deaf, or for any children with special needs, outside of Guadalajara, the state capital some 60 kilometres and a one hour bus ride north. Local schools frequently refused enrolment to deaf children, considered unteachable in their overcrowded classrooms. The two Canadians recognized the need for specialized help in this rural area and set about providing it. Word spread and soon a few more students began attending the little school. Volunteers were found to drive Ajijic children, soon four of them, the 17 kilometres back and forth each day.

Initially Roma and Jackie taught the small group of children themselves but, as more students arrived, they hired a local primary school teacher to help.

Lola Salamanca de Solís had little teaching experience and, like Roma and Jackie, no experience teaching the deaf. In a regular school she would have been addressed by first name only as *Maestra* Lola (Teacher Lola). Her deaf students called her simply Lola. Over time she learned to adapt her teaching methods to the needs of these children.

As Jackie wrote, "Every word must be taught by means of pictures or objects or actions, so visual aids are all-important." Jackie begged for funds and for magazines, picture books, toys, typewriters, watches and the like in frequent newsletters to Canada, in articles in the Lakeside press, and from everyone she met. She also made stacks of illustrated Spanish vocabulary cards, wrote and illustrated short story books about pueblo life written in very basic Spanish, and fashioned 3D cardboard objects to create a model pueblo and other simulated settings for themed language lessons. With Roma's help she even made a globe of the world, over a meter across, with the continents accurately mapped and mountain ranges raised in relief. Constructed of chicken wire and plaster of Paris, this globe, shown on the front

Hugs from Hermila at a party for teacher Lola Salamanca

cover, was extremely useful as a teaching aid and held together for over a decade.

Roma did a lot of the classroom teaching and introduced arts and crafts and, later, sewing and woodworking on Fridays to encourage communication and to develop useful skills. She also made sure there was a hot lunch served each day, prepared by student Rogelio's mother. Using her carpentry skills, she made much of the classroom furniture for the growing school, and provided transport for students as needed.

Classes ran from 10.00am to 5.00pm with breaks for lunch and outdoor play. "Mornings," wrote Jackie in 1980, "we concentrate on reading, writing, speech and lip-reading... and, in the afternoons, arts and crafts, typing, dancing, etc."

For any attempt to teach speech to deaf children, amplification is absolutely essential. Paul Messenger, a retired American hearing aid dealer, fitted the children with donated used hearing aids from a hearing aid bank organized by volunteers in Guadalajara. A used classroom amplification system was donated by the Indiana School for the Deaf early in the Jocotepec school's existence. A newspaper photo taken in 1981[2] shows about eight students seated at long tables, wearing large headphones, all linked together by the wired system to the teacher's microphone. This gave better amplification of the teacher's speech than the students' individual aids but required students to remain seated.

It was likely early 1981 when a young man from El Salvador visited the school and opened a new window to the world for the children. He knew American Sign Language and contributed three weeks of his time to introduce this visual language to the children and teachers. "The children became very excited with this new form of communication and learned "signing" rapidly."[3] A copy of the standard dictionary of American signs, *The Joy of Signing*, was obtained, and Jackie translated the English word titles into Spanish for teacher Lola, Roma and the students to continue expanding their signed vocabulary and their ability to communicate with each other.

Initial funding for the project

Jackie and Roma supported themselves from private incomes, but funds to operate the school needed to come from donations.[4] From the first months, there were costs for classroom supplies, for food, and for the small, almost token salary for the Mexican teacher. Moreover, Jackie and Roma had already initiated a second project—seeking assistance for physically disabled children in the area.

One day, probably in early 1980, Jackie was surprised to receive an envelope of small cheques from her son, Campbell, in British Columbia. Like his mother, Campbell felt the need to do something "to make a difference in the world." He had organized a fund-raising group among his friends, with each committing to 12 post-dated cheques a year. Some were only for five dollars monthly, but this first fund-raising effort meant a continuing source of cash was on hand. The cheques were made out to

"Mexican Kids Account." Thankfully, the local bank waived all fees for transactions for that account indefinitely.

Campbell's Canadian donor group grew substantially over the next four or five years, and was eventually sending hundreds of dollars a month as fund-raising events were added. His wife, Lianne, raised a large amount in sponsorships one year by running a marathon. Every few years Campbell drove to Lakeside with not just cheques but a van load of donated equipment.

Realizing the need for local input as well, Jackie and Roma persuaded friends in the Ajijic community to organize a support group. Jackie had written: "Teacher Lola has worked all year for US$60 a month. We need to pay her a proper salary." By January 1982 a committee with a slate of officers and "62 individual givers" had been formed.

Location, location, location

During the first two and a half years of its existence, the school moved from Jackie and Roma's home to three different locations in the town before finding a permanent home in a chicken coop.

In 1980 DIF Jocotepec, the local social service agency, offered a room in the municipal building on the plaza for free, but the children weren't happy there as it was dark and had no outdoor play area. So the following year, with enrolment of eight or nine students, they moved to a house with a garden, thanks to the rent being covered by one of the congregations at the Little Chapel in San Antonio Tlayacapan. Later, a Mexican business man donated the use of a large building, so the school moved again, only to have that building sold after six months as office space for the Electricity Company.

By then the Ajijic-based committee had begun fund-raising, and the decision was made to rent the large, floorless chicken coop and orchard behind Roma and Jackie's rented house on the highway at the eastern entrance to Jocotepec. The kindly Mexican

The school in the chicken coop, set in the middle of a former orchard

owner, Lola Urzúa, offered a three-year contract at a very modest
rent. Volunteers, both expatriate residents and snowbirds (visitors
from the north who stay for the winter), laboured for weeks in
early 1982 to convert the old chicken coop into two large, freshly
painted, airy rooms and a small kitchen.

Nearly 40 years later this building is still in use as part of the
enlarged Gallaudet Special Education Centre.

Inauguration of the Lakeside School for the Deaf

On Sunday March 21, 1982, about 100 people gathered at the
three-room school for the dedication of the renamed Lakeside
School for the Deaf (*Escuela Para Sordos de la Ribera*).

First, the nine or ten students presented a well-received skit,
narrated by short-term staff member, Canadian Leah Smith.
Then, in a brief ceremony, the Lakeside School for the Deaf, its
new building and grounds were dedicated in English by Elmo
Chatham, first president of the school committee, and in Spanish

by Sra. Guadalupe García, wife of the mayor of Jocotepec and president of DIF Jocotepec.

It was stressed that there would be no such school had it not been for Jackie and Roma who launched it all alone and had now inspired a real community project. Mr. Chatham emphasized that "the founders and co-directors of the school, Jackie Hartley and Roma Jones, should be recognized for their inspiration and faithful service."[5]

With the new committee now involved in fund-raising, Roma and Jackie had more time to work on their other project—bringing medical, rehabilitation and mobility services to physically disabled children— which they had initiated soon after starting the school. Again, there were no local services for these youngsters who were often found sitting or lying on a dirt floor in poverty-stricken homes.

This second project had Jackie and Roma regularly driving mothers and children to the Shriners Hospital in Mexico City, where the children could have free pediatric operations. The two Canadian women were constantly seeking appointments and reduced fees from hospitals in Guadalajara, while they dealt with the paperwork to import donated wheelchairs, crutches and braces. At any given time, they were actively seeking help for at least half a dozen children, many of them severely disabled. In the program's first four years, they arranged assessment and operations for more than two dozen children.

Long-time Jocotepec resident Joan Frost helped organize the medical consultations and transportation of equipment. Her one-woman fund-raising project, *Amigos de Salúd*, helped finance this and other local programs, including the Lakeside School.

2

The first specialist teachers

In the early summer of 1982, Jackie headed to British Columbia, Canada, for medical reasons, but also with a mission. The new committee had authorized Jackie to seek a trained teacher of the deaf willing to volunteer for a year at the Lakeside School. Teacher Lola was expecting her first child and would be on maternity leave from November. There were simply no Mexican specialist teachers of the deaf in the region, so the success of Jackie's search would be pivotal for the future growth of the school.

In Vancouver, Jackie contacted the University of British Columbia (UBC) which offered a training program for teachers of the deaf and hard of hearing. Susan van Gurp and I had just completed that program when we met with her. We garnered only limited information about the school and the town, but Jackie's views on education seemed up-to-date and her boundless enthusiasm for the project was persuasive. On offer was an exciting professional challenge with no guarantees. We decided to take a chance and head south for a year, starting in September. Susan had once vacationed in Mexico and, as it happened, had actually passed through Jocotepec. I had never been to Mexico and knew little about the country.

The salary was to be US$100 a month each, which turned out to be less than the minimum salary for the (poorly paid) teachers in government schools and barely enough to cover basic living expenses. Jackie mentioned that the committee had asked her to find one teacher, not two, but she was convinced that life in traditional Jocotepec would be too difficult for one woman alone, so she invited both of us along on the adventure. As a result, faced with two air fares and salaries for two, the committee ran out of money by the end of October and had to borrow from a supporter to pay our third month's salary.

Before leaving Vancouver, I undertook an intensive summer course in conversational Spanish at UBC and Susan dusted-off her notes from an earlier university Spanish course. We were fortunate to receive a donation of reconditioned wireless classroom amplifiers and with these group hearing aids, our Spanish grammar books, and words of encouragement from UBC staff, we flew to Mexico.

Jocotepec in 1982

Our new hometown was a traditional Mexican pueblo, with *burros* and cows sometimes wandering the cobblestone streets while Mexican *rancheros* on horseback wove between fume-belching buses. The streets were always full of children, playing hopscotch or marbles, since they attended either a morning school or an afternoon session. Nearly every corner had a vendor selling roasted corn or *garbanzo* beans, crispy *churritos* sprinkled with lime and chili or other home-made snacks. Along the main street were small stores with limited stock, some specializing in one craft like sombreros or leather sandals. On the side streets, during harvest season, you might find the pavement occupied by a layer of beans, spread out to dry in the sun in front of a humble dwelling. There was a busy daily indoor market selling freshly-butchered meat, fish from the lake, local fruits and vegetables, handmade *piñatas*, and orange or carrot juice squeezed while you waited and served in a take-away plastic bag with a straw.

Most of the houses were single-story adobe, many missing large patches of plaster, their frontages built right along the pavement.

Like our house, they might date from the mid-1800s. Looking into doorways as you walked by was always a pleasurable surprise—the inner courtyards could contain a tradesman's workshop or a tropical garden or, towards the back, a pen to hold the family cow overnight. Homeowners were responsible for construction of the pavement in front of the residence. Hence, you needed to watch your steps as a slippery tiled section might be followed by rough concrete or a broken stone surface, all at different heights and slopes. The occupant of the home was also responsible for street cleaning, so early morning would find the women sweeping the street in front of their house, often sloshing a bucket of water over the road to dampen the dust temporarily.

The large town plaza, the centre of social life, had an ornate bandstand and lots of wrought iron seating shaded by leafy trees. Sunday nights, with the band playing, the plaza was packed with local families, from toddlers to grandparents, everyone dressed in their best outfit. The teenage boys and young men circled around the plaza in one direction, while the girls, arm-in-arm with friends and sisters, circled the other way. A boy might trade a rose for a *vuelta*—a turn around the plaza with the girl of his choice—if she agreed.

At one corner of the plaza was a small supermarket. Inside were the only two public phones in the town. Calls were placed old-style by a telephone operator. Wait times were usually lengthy as there were very few private phones in the community; even some doctors' clinics had no phone due to a dire shortage of new lines to the town. It wasn't until the early 1990s that the Lakeside School could obtain a telephone line.

Next to the plaza was the main church. From its tower, bells rang out reminding parishioners to hurry to mass, and a powerful public address system boomed out announcements about the time of a funeral service, football schedules, lost property and appeals for help to locate a lost child. The school made use of this free service on many occasions.

Arrival of the new teachers

An early newsletter from the school committee introduced readers at Lakeside, and in Canada and the US, to their newly-appointed Canadian teachers and welcomed us to the school:

> Gwen Chan and Susan van Gurp each hold postgraduate diplomas in education of the deaf from UBC. Gwen has taught special education students in Melbourne (Australia) and Toronto and deaf students in Vancouver. Susan has worked with emotionally disturbed adolescents and deaf and deaf-blind children in Canada. These two teachers earned in excess of $38,000 and $25,000 annually in Canada. So you can see they are highly trained and experienced. We are indeed fortunate to have them working with our children this year.

Susan and I lived in Jackie and Roma's house for the first two months. There was no water for the first week because, Jackie explained, "Some fool diverted the water pipe a week ago." Introductory visits to some of the committee members' homes provided all of us with much-needed showers.

It was only a short walk from the backdoor of the house to the three-room school, through the old orchard of avocado, mango and citrus trees. We held classes in the largest room and part of the kitchen, since the other room was set up for carpentry, crafts and general storage. The rooms were clean and white, newly painted earlier in the year before the school's inauguration. On both sides of the building were large windows that had no glass or security bars, just chicken wire. It would be many years before the school could afford the luxury of sliding glass windows. In the meantime, we were sometimes shivery cold in January and suffered from the dust storms in the hot, dry, windy season before the rains arrived in June or July.

When we started teaching in September 1982, there were nine deaf students attending, aged 6 to 14, plus several other children with physical disabilities or language delay. Susan and I convinced Jackie that future enrolments should be limited to deaf students. Academic classes started at 8:30am. Students shared a hot lunch together and stayed for crafts and vocational training in the afternoons, taught by Roma and volunteers.

The first week, we began assessing the children's math, reading and writing levels. Susan and I were far from fluent in Spanish on arrival; however, it was easy to stay ahead of the students in language proficiency. Besides, teacher Lola Salamanca was able to help us until she started her maternity leave in November. There were no student audiograms on file but fortunately there was a used audiometer which Campbell had bought in Victoria, B.C "for a fraction of its retail cost." So we began testing the children's hearing, prior to making molds and fitting the FM classroom aids.

The students' big "news" in our first weeks came one morning when they arrived excitedly signing that there was a dead cow on the road in front of Jackie's house. Of course this gave us a great opportunity for some new language work around the incident. Apparently, the cow had been hit by a truck overnight. By law, the driver was supposed to cut off the ear with the identification tag and take it to the police station. The owner of the cow would be liable for any damages since the cow was not supposed to be on the road.

After some months at the school, Susan and I reported back to fellow teachers in BC about our initial experience teaching at the Lakeside School. The article was subsequently published in a professional newsletter:

> Considering most of the children have had a maximum of two years schooling and most are profoundly deaf, their communication skills are fairly well developed. The program we have initiated is similar to ... Total Communication programs in Canada and USA. However, in our curriculum planning we have had to take into account the limited educational background of the students. We are trying to select the infor-

Susan van Gurp teaching Hermila and Mario 1984

mation, concepts and skills which will be most useful to the older students, who are almost of working age and unlikely to remain in school for long.

The students are a joy to teach—hungry for information, mature in their attitudes and displaying a great sense of humour. They participate enthusiastically in school activities from mime to janitorial chores, to chasing the frequently wandering cows out of the school yard with shouts of '*Vaca, vaca*' (cow) as they stream out of the classroom.

Although we lack the sophisticated teaching aids and support services of Canadian schools, we are finding it surprisingly easy to improvise effectively.... The students have responded well to the FM hearing aids and speech training and... we are noticing improvement in their spoken language.[6]

In addition to our classroom responsibilities, we began searching for other deaf children by visiting local villages with Roma or Jackie and asking the priest to tell their parishioners about the school. In Ixtlahuacán de los Membrillos, a village near Chapala, a trainee teacher had searched out every child with a disability in the village and had written his mandatory thesis on the topic. Jackie was informed of this and, in December 1983, Susan and her visiting brother, Dr. Gerald van Gurp, accompanied Jackie to investigate what services might be needed. Amongst the children whom the teacher had located, they found three deaf youngsters— Juan Diego, 5, Esther 15, Juan Carlos, 8—and Juan Carlos' deaf mother, María, 33. Arrangements were made for all to attend the Lakeside School in the New Year. Thus, by early 1984, enrolment had grown to 16 deaf students, ranging in age from 5 to 33.

Susan and I were also the school's social workers. One of our new students, a bright 17-year-old girl from a nearby village, was suddenly absent after attending daily for months. She smuggled a note, hidden in her bra, to another of our teenage girls from the same Lakeside town to give to her teacher, Susan. The note begged Susan to come and talk with her father and included the bus fare. Susan found the father was having a feud with the family of the other deaf student and didn't want his daughter associating with members of that family. Susan did a lot of "sweet talking" with both families and our new student returned to classes.

For new students and their teachers, the first few months at school were always very exciting. We watched shy, uncommunicative children and adolescents blossom with the ability to communicate through sign language and, in some cases, speech. Their worlds opened up so quickly. The small enrolment and mixed-age classes fostered a family atmosphere at the school and without exception the students all loved coming to school. 16-year-old Mario, one of the original students from Ajijic, only missed one day in 1984 and he had a good excuse—he was in jail overnight!

To provide the students with new experiences and an expanded vocabulary for language work, we took small groups on local field trips. Additionally, thanks to local supporters, the students were soon able to enjoy some horseback riding sessions in Chapala and, for many years, bi-weekly swimming classes in Jocotepec.

In 1983 we took all the students on a memorable excursion to the centre of Guadalajara, a city of 2.5 million inhabitants. Although it was barely an hour away, none of them had been there before. In the up-scale department store, Salinas y Rocha, with decor of stainless steel and mirrors, the wide-eyed students were introduced to an escalator and an elevator. It took many tries before they were confident enough to ride the escalator and, once at the top, teenage Felicitas took Susan's hand and placed it on her chest to show her how fast her heart was beating. They had to go up and down a few times before we could move on and take the elevator to the second floor. Later that day, we whizzed-up to the top of the Sheraton Hotel for a view over the city. With shaky legs, they could hardly walk afterwards.

The varied histories of some of the students enrolled in the first five years are featured in chapter 4: Veronica who became a teaching assistant; Francisca, a smart 11-year-old who could only write her name after four years in a local primary school but who quickly learned to read; Felicitas, her frightened 17-year-old sister, who couldn't recognize her own name in print or speech on arrival; mother and son, María and Juan Carlos, who needed a way to communicate with each other; Carmela, who later graduated from secondary school; and María Elena, our first boarding student, aged 5.

Precarious finances

The Lakeside School was operating on a shoestring budget in the early 1980s and, obviously, long term financial stability was needed to secure the future of the school. So, after six months on the job, Susan and I decided we should attempt to obtain grants from international foundations.

Neither of us had ever seen a grant application, let alone written one. However, we were so immersed in the school project that we just wrote from the heart about the need for the little, atypical school in the chicken coop to continue to operate, since there was

no alternative education available for current or future students
so desperately in need of help.

With assistance from Susan's brother, Gerald, who was on the
board of the Montreal YMCA, our pleas were sent to dozens of
foundations in Canada, the US and Europe, with a cover letter
from the Montreal YMCA. Our first response came from the
Executive Director of the huge Public Welfare Foundation in
Washington DC. She requested that we call her collect, which we
did from the phone in the tiny supermarket. After we answered a
few questions, she told us that she'd been nearly in tears reading
our description of the school and the students, and that she would
be forwarding a cheque for US$5000.

Some months later, the Clifford E. Lee Foundation in Canada
responded with a Cnd$3000 donation. Thanks to the YMCA's
connections, this second bonanza was multiplied six times within
Canada before deposit to the school account. (chapter 12)

A house for Susan and Gwen

Our home, after the first few months, was a 110-year-old house on
the main street, with five rooms facing into a large interior courtyard
and garden where we could lounge, plan lessons and study Spanish.
Thankfully, we house-sat rent free. But the property had not been
maintained, so, before moving in, Roma, Susan and I spent our
afternoons for two weeks plastering holes in the interior adobe,
whitewashing the walls and spraying the woven reed matting on the
ceilings to reduce the resident population of scorpions and insects.

The living room roof leaked buckets during the rainy season
and there was no hot water in the kitchen. Neither was there a
tinaco—the typical rooftop water storage tank that was filled by
electric pump when the municipal water was flowing in your area
of the town. Without that, we were at the mercy of a 12-hours-a-
day water supply on an irregular schedule. Washing clothes in the
concrete trough was always risky as the flow of water might stop at

any minute. But the old house was spacious and we soon adopted a somewhat traditional Mexican life-style.

Susan and I had signed on to teach for one year, but found both the challenges and the rewards so great that we stayed for a second year and continued living in our old Mexican house. By mid-1984 Susan, Lola and I were feeling very positive about the progress each of our 16 students was making with their ability to communicate, and with their growing self-confidence and self-esteem, fostered by the friendly, family atmosphere at the school.

Roma continued to organize small-group, afternoon classes, with a vocational skills emphasis, with the help of a few volunteers from the North American community. The girls were proud of the dresses and blouses they made in afternoon sewing classes. Teenagers Juan and Mario learned carpentry from Roma who also taught craft classes and, for a while, gave cooking classes to the girls in the new kitchen. Jackie continued to create Spanish language educational materials for the classroom and never missed an opportunity to solicit help for the school from near and far.

By the end of our second school year, Susan had decided to return to Canada. The committee's newsletter opened with the news:

> We are sorry to announce the departure of Susan van Gurp after her two years of very fruitful service at the school. Susan has accepted a teaching position at the prestigious Montreal Oral School. We wish her well and thank her heartily for her loving and energetic work with the students of the Lakeside School.... Gwen Chan will be with us for the first few months of the new school year in order to continue training our new local teacher, Sara, and to give Susan's replacement, a newly graduated teacher of the deaf from the US, a chance to settle in smoothly.

Back in Canada, Susan van Gurp started teaching at the Montreal Oral School for the Deaf in the fall of 1984 and went on to teach pre-schoolers at the Vancouver Oral Centre and various age groups at the BC School for the Deaf. She earned her Ph.D. in Educational Psychology and Special Education in 1997 and taught in university teacher training programs in California and British Columbia, Canada. After a career of 28 years in the education of deaf students, Susan retired from a position as Principal, British Columbia School for the Deaf, in Burnaby, BC, in 2010. She now divides her time between her Mexican home in Baja California Sur and her daughter's home in Vancouver, BC.

Because the smooth transition of staff envisaged for September-October 1984 did not work out as planned (chapter 7), I stayed on at the Lakeside School until Christmas that year before flying north to Montreal to teach in the Mackay Centre for the Deaf.

Susan and I were both in Montreal in 1985, when we heard of the horrific assault on Roma. One night in mid-June that year, Roma's former gardener arrived at the house, high on some drug, and demanded money and the keys to her car. When Roma told him she would help him if he returned in the morning, he pulled out a knife and stabbed her numerous times in the abdomen and arm. Roma almost died while Jackie frantically tried to wake anyone in town with access to a phone. It took hours for the Red Cross ambulance to arrive from Chapala to take Roma to Guadalajara where she underwent many hours of surgery late that night.

Weeks later, she was able to fly to Canada for further operations and rehabilitation; she was not well enough to return to Jocotepec until December that year. Jackie, meanwhile, had handed over all administration of the school to the committee and was concentrating her efforts on the program for the physically disabled and on completing renovations to a different rented house in time for Roma's return just before Christmas.

My appointment as director

In August 1985, at the request of the Board of Directors, I returned to the school as director, to teach alongside teachers Citlali, Sara and Lola and two teaching assistants-in-training, Veronica and Rita, recently appointed by Jackie. The teachers had experienced some interpersonal conflicts in my absence, and Roma and Jackie had had major disagreements with some members of the Board, so I arrived with some trepidation about the future. However, everyone welcomed me back and staff declared they could cooperate with each other again. Twenty students were enrolled when classes began in September and the school was about to start its unique boarding program. There was still no hope of obtaining a telephone line in the school or at my new home and there was now no vehicle available for school use.

I rented a small house a few blocks from the school in one of the poorer barrios of Jocotepec where the rent was quite cheap. This house, unlike the one Susan and I had shared, did have a permanent water supply and hot water in the tiny kitchen and bathroom: however, I was without a refrigerator for a month as, when the new one was delivered, it had no Freon gas in it.

Farewell to Jackie and Roma

In June 1986 the school and community held a farewell ceremony at the school for Jackie and Roma, who were moving back to Victoria, British Columbia, because of Jackie's deteriorating health. A brass plaque was unveiled commemorating the founding of the Lakeside School for the Deaf by Jackie Hartley and Roma Jones in 1979. Their final gift to the school was a large, hand-made, furnished doll house for the kindergarten classroom.

In Victoria, the two ladies finally had time to pursue their artistic interests in painting and crafts, sometimes exhibiting and selling their creations. They stayed in close contact with the school and are remembered at Lakeside as two Canadians who truly made a difference in the lives of Mexican children.

3

Students from far afield

For some Mexican families, deafness, or any disability, was something to be ashamed of, to be kept secret. For others, it was God's will; they believed, fatalistically, that nothing could be done for such a child. Thankfully, many families did actively seek help and education for their deaf child, whilst others could at least be persuaded to consider the opportunities offered by education at the school.

Where did students come from?

When Susan and I arrived in September 1982, three years after Jackie and Roma started teaching, the students came from Jocotepec or the village of Ajijic, 20 kilometres east along the lake, with two exceptions—Juan came from Zapotitán, 12 kilometres north, and 11-year-old Hermila travelled for an hour by bus from Chapala each morning.

A decade later, the school was educating students from towns, villages and tiny *ranchos* up to 125 kilometres (78 miles) away and providing weekly home-based boarding for more than half of the 42–44 students attending classes. Bus travel was very expensive relative to the basic wage and, apart from the problem of the cost, all the boarding students had to negotiate the schedules of two or three bus companies en route to school, making daily trips from home impossible in terms of the hours of travel involved. Two major

Jocotepec with Lake Chapala and Cerro García behind (Photo by John Frost)

bus companies had end-of-line bus stations in Jocotepec with routes to Guadalajara, one running east through Chapala, and the other going north on Highway 80, both enabling connections to a web of rural bus lines. The school's location at this transport hub was an important factor in its ability to serve students from such a wide area.

During the 1980s, several families moved to Jocotepec from Guadalajara and other communities to be close to the services offered to their deaf child or children at the Lakeside School. Two families were able to return to their home towns at Lakeside from California after hearing from relatives about the school.

The map at the start of the book shows the home towns, or nearest settlement, of all the Lakeside School students from 1979–1994.

How did parents hear about the school?

Many families learned of the school by word of mouth from parents in their village or a neighbouring village. From the town of Arenal came 5-year-old María Elena in 1983, then 6-year-old Armando in 1985 and 4-year-old Mario in 1986.

Sometimes, staff would make an afternoon trip to a village where there was rumoured to be a deaf child, or to a town where we thought there were likely to be deaf children given the size of the community. If there was a local school, we would ask for their help. But, since deaf children were unlikely to be enrolled, that seldom gave us any leads. We would talk to the local priest who would usually agree to publicize the existence of the school in announcements at mass. Simply asking random women on the street if they knew "where the deaf child lived, the one who cannot speak", occasionally led us to families with a hidden deaf child, or at least a non-verbal child.

In larger centres, DIF social workers eventually learned of the school as it became more widely known. This was the referral source for the four children in family M. from a distant municipality in 1992. Various children's social services in Guadalajara also referred families to the school or sent us children, some of whom, like Pedro X, arrived without any advance notice.

Sometimes, it took time and patience to persuade parents to enrol their deaf children. Three sisters started at Lakeside School in January 1991; one of their brothers joined them in September. They came from a small village close to the Guadalajara airport, about 65 kilometres from Jocotepec. Their parents heard about the school from one of our students in a nearby village. Their modest concrete block house was part of a dusty family compound of three homes where chickens, ducks and a few animals roamed freely amongst the clotheslines and outdoor washing troughs. The father was a truck driver, and the family had six children aged 4 to 17, four of them with hearing loss.

The children's mother first came to the school in October 1990 and promised to bring the girls to see the school the following week. They didn't arrive. It took three visits by staff to their home over the following months before the parents could be convinced that their daughters would be safe boarding in Jocotepec. Each time, the Señora was in tears throughout the visit. The three girls eventually arrived after Christmas and were all boarded with a loving local family consisting of three young hearing children, a truck-driver father, and a mother who had learned Mexican sign language whilst caring for other deaf students in past years. The girls settled happily into their "second home" after some tears the first few days away from the family.

Their mother, realizing the girls really wanted to come to school and were safe and happy with their new "family", was able to appear at school by the third week, smiling instead of weepy-eyed, bearing gifts of eggs for the daily school snack, and a collection of glasses and cups (stamped Mexicana Airlines) for the foster house where crockery was in short supply. She was obviously pleased that the girls were finally receiving help, even if it meant being away from home four nights a week—her sacrifice had been rewarded.

The incidence of deafness among Mexican children

One of the questions most frequently asked by visitors to the Lakeside School was, "Are there more deaf children in this area than you'd find in a Canadian or US population of similar size? Is the incidence of deafness amongst children here higher than normal?"

In the 1980s, I think the answer was probably "Yes." I have no local research statistics to corroborate my hunch; what follows is mainly based on my knowledge of the personal and family backgrounds of our students.

The tradition of large families in Mexico at that time often resulted in families having more than one deaf child. The Lakeside School had many students with deaf siblings. Of the more than 110 students over the years, at least seven families had two deaf children, one family had three, and three families each had four deaf children at the school. These were all families with hearing parents, with just one exception; deaf siblings Viviana and José, of Ajijic, had a deaf mother and Viviana would later have a deaf son.

Our "one big happy family" at recess

In Canada, with two-child families the norm, it would have been extremely rare to find three or four deaf siblings in a family in the 1980s or '90s. Given that large families were common in Mexico, it was not surprising that our families with three or four deaf children would have another two, three, four or more hearing children at home as well.

The majority of our students were profoundly deaf; even with a powerful hearing aid they could not hear all the sounds of speech well enough to understand spoken language. Most could hear loud environmental sounds and perhaps the bass beat of loud music with their hearing aids turned on. Others, with lesser but still severe hearing loss, could learn to communicate orally within a limited vocabulary, given hearing aids and intensive speech and language instruction, depending on how old they were when they arrived at the school.

Some of the children we helped had moderate hearing loss caused, not by genetics, but by chronic middle ear infections in early childhood that were untreated or unresponsive to available treatment. With a hearing aid, and some short-term intensive speech and language teaching, they were often able to integrate into regular primary school classes. The incidence of chronic middle ear infection has been seen, by some experts, as a useful indicator of the level of development of the public health care system in a nation.

Other untreated medical problems also contributed to a higher than normal incidence of hearing loss. Two young siblings, Angelica and Eduardo, were living on a remote farm as young children when the whole family contracted a serious illness accompanied by very high fever. The family was unable to access medical assistance. Particularly in rural Mexico, many families lacked good quality medical care because of distance or cost, or both. After recovery, the two children were found to have severe, permanent hearing loss, due to damage to the cochlea. Thankfully, they joined our school as boarders for five years and were bright and successful students.

Communication and educational level on enrolment

Formal sign language was unknown in the region prior to the existence of the Lakeside School. Deaf children and deaf adults had always just used home-made signs and gestures to try to communicate basic needs within the family. Only in the largest cities, like Guadalajara and Mexico City, was Mexican Sign Language known and used by the adult deaf population, who belonged to social organizations for the deaf and thus had the possibility of communicating fully with their family and deaf friends.

With few exceptions, when new students began they could not read any written words except, perhaps, their name—regardless of their age or how many years of public schooling they had attended. Some really bright children had moved with their peers through Grade 4 in their village school, copying neatly from the blackboard or a classmate's notes, but were unable to understand the Spanish text.

Mexican schools taught basic reading in Grade 1 entirely by the phonetic method, sounding out words the children already understood letter by letter. Children with hearing loss had no chance of cracking this code, as the jumble of letters held no meaning for them. A few of the brighter students, however, had managed to master some arithmetic, at least to a Grade 2 level, as mathematics is not as dependent on the ability to hear and understand spoken language. The only student who arrived at the Lakeside School with some knowledge of Mexican Sign Language, and a small reading vocabulary, was Ivonne, who for the previous few years had attended a school for the deaf in Mexico City where, of course, the teaching of reading was not based on a phonetic approach.

Many of our students had never attended any school or kindergarten and some, of school age, seemed never to have even handled a pencil or coloured with crayons. New students were usually ignorant of time concepts (like weeks, months, minutes), monetary values and even who's-who relationships within the extended family. They could neither ask nor answer "who, why, when, where and how" about their daily life, let alone comprehend the concepts of a wider world.

Only a very few profoundly deaf, intelligent young adults, like José M., had learned at home to tell the time, manage money, use a tape measure and make their needs known by gestures even though they were unable to read, write or speak before enrolling at the school.

Years of education at the Lakeside School

At the end of the school year in June 1994, about 30 of the students then attending had fewer than five years of education at the Lakeside School. Another 12 had been students for six years or more. For two young teenagers it was their ninth and tenth year in attendance respectively.

For hearing children in rural Mexico, completing Grade 6 at primary school was still considered quite an achievement in the 1980s. A Grade 6 certificate was accepted by many poor and working-class families as the termination of a child's formal education, especially for girls. These families often needed their adolescent children, once literate, to contribute financially, often as extra help with the family farm or small business. In the case of girls, large families meant help was always needed with household chores and perhaps the care of younger siblings.

Unfortunately, these societal norms affected the expectations of many of our families with deaf children. The first two children that Jackie and Roma began teaching in late 1979, Rogelio and Aurora, were no longer in attendance a few years later. Rogelio, by then 12 years old, had begun working with his father in his trucking business, while Aurora helped out at home. However, the majority of our students starting as school-age children did manage to attend classes for at least four or five years. After several years of intensive, small-group, specialized teaching, even those who arrived with no formal language—signed, spoken or written—were finally able to understand and ask questions; attain a basic level of reading and writing; master enough practical math for daily use; gain an understanding of many abstract concepts like the calendar, the clock and the location of Mexico on planet Earth; and learn some history, science, health and vocational skills.

Even if they would have benefited from additional years in school, by the time they left our students had acquired new levels of literacy, worldly knowledge and vocational skills. They had also all developed positive feelings about themselves and their own abilities.

They valued the friendships their new communication skills had enabled them to form in their deaf community at school and in the wider world. Today, many use Facebook as one way to keep in touch with deaf and hearing friends and family.

4

Individual stories: First students, 1979–1984

Here are stories of some of the students who enrolled in the first five years of the school's existence.

Veronica, our first deaf teaching assistant

Veronica was born into a large and poor family in Ajijic. She had nine siblings. Her father was a bus driver, her mother a maid. From age 7, Veronica, who had a severe hearing loss, was one of the three or four children who attended after-school speech classes twice weekly in the mid-to-late 1970s with Lyn Hallinger in Ajijic.

Following Lyn's departure, Veronica, aged 10, became one of the first students to enrol in Jackie and Roma's new school for the deaf in Jocotepec in 1979. There, the addition of sign language allowed Veronica to communicate with her Mexican teacher, Lola, and with fellow students as she learned to read and write basic Spanish and developed her spoken vocabulary over five years of classes.

With her sunny, outgoing personality, Veronica was always popular with her peers and helpful with younger students. In 1985, Jackie suggested she begin training as the first teaching assistant in the growing school. She was often assigned to help teach new students their first Mexican signs and first written words. Our kindergarten students worked well with Veronica because she was firm but flexible, creative and enthusiastic and, of course, she knew what it's like to be deaf.

In 1990 Veronica joined teachers Citlali and Lupita on a two-week visit to the Indiana School for the Deaf. There she observed highly qualified teachers and teaching assistants, both deaf and hearing, working in a large, well-equipped residential school.

At home, having been unwilling to learn sign language, her family communicated orally with Veronica, and her mother was satisfied that she and Veronica understood each other. With strangers, communication was more limited, though Veronica could read and write enough Spanish to get a message across. Unfortunately, the school lost Veronica's helpful service when she moved to Guadalajara with her mother.

Carmela, who needed a very special hearing aid

Carmela, from Jocotepec, was one of the first children to join the new school in 1980. She had a moderate hearing loss, associated with a syndrome that included a lack of normal ear canals. Her sweet, softly spoken, illiterate mother provided Carmela with little or no language stimulus; on arrival at the school at age 5, she had a spoken vocabulary of only half a dozen words. With amplification and individualized small group teaching, she began the long process of catching-up with her hearing peers.

A big break for Carmela came when the Canadian International Hearing Services procured a bone conduction aid especially designed for her by clinician Peter Keller in Toronto. This aid, held against the skull by a metal headband, together with a powerful hearing aid pinned to her blouse (and disguised as a brooch), transmitted sound by vibration and allowed Carmela to hear speech fairly clearly.

Eventually, Carmela could speak and read well enough to be successfully integrated into Grade 2 in a regular primary school. She graduated from junior high school (quite an achievement for

With communication came friendship: (L-R) Hermila, Francisca, Socorro, Veronica, Felicitas

any local girl in those days) and later attended a commercial academy. Carmela married José M., an economically successful former student (and former employee of the Lakeside School), and they have brought up two hearing children, living in the house that José built for them on his family's farm.

Felicitas and Francisca

Felicitas and Francisca, two sisters from the neighbouring town of San Juan Cosalá, arrived at the school in March 1983 and joined Susan van Gurp's class of new students.

Felicitas, then 17, was so profoundly deaf that even a hearing aid was of no real help to her. She was timid, too frightened to try anything new, and with no way of communicating her feelings except by tears. Over-protected at home, she had spent her life sweeping and washing in a household of 13 people. Meanwhile her younger, more outgoing, severely deaf sister, Francisca, had attended classes at the local elementary school. Francisca, aged 11 when the two girls started, at first did everything for her dependent older sister—guided her activities, answered for her, helped with her drawings and paid her bus fare.

Like many of our deaf school-age students, Felicitas came to us unable to pronounce, print or read her own name, unable to count out 5 pesos, and with no means of communication except for some basic home-made signs. She had been given no language for important abstract concepts like "next week, December, always, perhaps", or for emotions, or for relationship distinctions like "sisters, cousins or friends."

Nine months after her enrolment, Felicitas' teacher said, "I would not have imagined that the experience of coming to a school for the deaf could so dramatically change the personality of an older adolescent in so short a time."

Three years later, both girls had made amazing progress. Felicitas could confidently entertain her deaf friends in sign language with humorous stories of what happened on the weekend. She understood our arbitrary system of naming and ordering days and months. She could tell us what time her bus left, and could manage small amounts of money, like counting out coins to pay her bus fare. Learning to read and write proved difficult for Felicitas, but this did not affect her ever-growing confidence in herself.

Younger sister Francisca had also made remarkable strides. In her local school she had moved with her peers through to Grade 4 before transferring to our school. Severely deaf, without a hearing aid or specialized instruction, she could only copy words from the blackboard, and sum to 10. Despite being very intelligent, she couldn't read even simple words and had not developed spoken language.

In three years of small-group teaching and specialized methods, Francisca had made rapid progress. When a class for the hearing impaired in Pennsylvania initiated pen pal contact with our students, Francisca, 15 , answered her very first letter.

She proudly wrote, solo, a letter describing her family, her father's occupation, her jobs at home and her favourite activities. She could read and write simple sentences in past, present and future tenses. With the help of her hearing aid and lip reading, she could understand simple spoken statements and had developed intelligible speech within a limited vocabulary. With sign language she was able to ask questions about her world, tell what she dreamt of last night, and even express her feelings and opinions. She was a delightful, well adjusted, intelligent and independent teenager, with a bright future.

Indeed, when she was 18, we employed Francisca as our teaching assistant to work with the junior kindergarten children, helping them to learn sign language and to have success in all the usual pre-school activities. Francisca was a wonderful role model for our students—a young deaf lady with a paying job and the respect of all the staff.

Felicitas, too, was employed at the school for a couple of years as our cook. With guidance from teacher Linda, she was responsible for preparing drinks and a nutritious snack for everyone in time for morning recess. At her next place of employment she made use of the dressmaking skills she had learned at school, working with an older sister in a home-based business.

María Elena, our first boarding student

One Monday afternoon in October 1983, Sra. V., from Arenal—the gateway to the blue agave region of Tequila—arrived with her 5-year-old daughter, María Elena, seeking information about a rumoured school for the deaf in Jocotepec. Jackie convinced her to leave María Elena in her care that same day, and to come back for her on Friday.

Susan and I were aghast at the decision, fearing that the little girl would feel abandoned, and maybe traumatized, since no one had prepared her for this sudden change. She had only the clothes she was wearing, and there was no way we could let her understand that her mother would return to collect her from these strangers on Friday. However, María Elena proved us wrong. She seemed unperturbed, ate and slept well that first night and, once classes started in the morning, was one happy, enthusiastic young student.

For the next two school years, María Elena lived with Jackie, Roma and two other children that they were caring for. María Elena returned to Arenal every Friday afternoon to spend three nights at home. One of 10 children, the family sometimes found it difficult to pay the bus fares for María Elena and an older sibling to travel the 90 kilometres to and from Jocotepec twice a week.

María Elena began boarding with a local Mexican family in September 1985 and continued happily living with them for the next eight years. Sra. Evelia Moreno, her host mother, and her young daughters, Lilia and Rocío, learned to sign quite well. Several neighbourhood children ventured to Saturday morning sign classes because they wanted to be able to communicate better with María Elena who was a popular participant in the local kids' activities. As teenagers, Lilia would sometimes spend the weekend with María Elena's family in Arenal and, decades later, they still maintain a sisterly friendship.

One Saturday in February 1987, when María Elena and fellow boarder, little Mario from Arenal, were unable to return home for the weekend, I took them and Lilia and Rocío to the Chili Cook-Off in Ajijic. This was, and still is, an annual outdoor entertainment and fund-raising event with the Lakeside School being one of the beneficiaries. On the way back we called in on Jean Carmichael, then president of the school committee. She encouraged the children to select a few items each of quality used clothing from the large stack donated for the students by parishioners in Albany, New York. Next we stopped at my small house in Jocotepec so they could enjoy taking a warm shower. This was a luxury for all four as neither Sra. Evelia nor the families in Arenal could afford to install a hot water heater in their bathroom.

In a letter to María Elena's North American sponsor in 1988, we reported that:

> At age 10, María Elena is a bright child with a sunny, inde-
> pendent personality and, being very attractive, is frequently
> photographed by visitors. Although profoundly deaf, she has
> a pleasant natural voice and has developed some intelligible
> speech. She's proud to be able to read and write basic Spanish
> and enjoys learning about the wider world. She is always lov-
> ing and helpful and a favourite of students and teachers alike.
> She has lately taken to running up and giving each teacher a
> goodbye kiss on the cheek before leaving school each day.

María Elena earned her Grade 6 certificate before leaving school. Having done well in the school's dressmaking courses for some years, she found employment in commercial clothing pro-duction before becoming self-employed as a dressmaker working out of the family home. She now divides her time between Arenal and California where some family members live.

Juan Carlos and his mother, María

The short biographies in this book are all based on my personal knowledge of the students. The story of Juan Carlos and his mother is presented in more detail because I had a more personal connection to them. Juan Carlos stayed with me on weekdays for nearly two years. His story is a somewhat extreme example of the problems that can arise when a child grows up both deaf and severely socially-disadvantaged.

Juan Carlos was aged 8 and his severely deaf mother, María, 33, when we located them in the distant village of Ixtlahuacán de los Membrillos in December 1983. Juan Carlos was profoundly deaf, tall, thin and unschooled. According to the village priest, he was ridiculed by the local boys and spent his days alone, scrounging in garbage cans. His mother knew no sign language, could not read or write, and her speech was largely unintelligible. Between mother and son there could be little communication. They lived in a one-room, dirt-floor dwelling and María's inadequate income was earned caring for the animals on a nearby farm. Arrangements were made for them both to start classes the following January.

When Juan Carlos (JC) first arrived at school, his attitude to everything new was: I don't know how and I'm too scared to try. He burst into tears if his wishes were not met immediately. He would not sit in a chair, but crawled under the table or wandered around hiding everything in sight, making annoying sounds and looking very frightened. But, within a few months, he was a different child. He was so glad to be at school each day I nicknamed him "Happiness Himself." He was increasingly affectionate with his mother and the staff, sometimes smiling shyly as he touched a teacher's arm.

Two years later, both JC and his mother had changed dramatically. María, with a hearing aid and two years of daily speech, language and life skills training with teacher Lola, could now be understood when she spoke. She and JC could communicate in basic sign language about the "how, when and where" of their daily activities, so JC no longer burst into tears of frustration because of his inability to understand what was happening.

Once she was able to converse more freely, María was seen to be a friendly, warmhearted woman who really cared about her son. She and JC could finally laugh and play together. With some monetary help from Canadian sponsors, and payment to María for after-class janitorial work at the school, María and J.C. were managing much better. JC always looked clean and had eaten breakfast before taking the bus for the 75-minute ride to school with his mother.

JC loved pouring over *National Geographic* magazines, liked studying insects and enjoyed painting. After two years of classes he could read a few very simple sentences, knew the order of the days of the week, was learning to tell the time and could add and subtract

Juan Carlos celebrating his mother's birthday in 1986

to ten. He needed lots of praise and reassurance in the classroom but was, in turn, an affectionate and happy-natured 10-year-old.

He could also be a great ambassador for the school. One afternoon, I had to take 10-year-old JC with me to an Ajijic cocktail party because there was no one else available to look after him. Ted Fisher, our host and past-president of the Board, had not seen JC since his early, wild days at the school. Told that JC would be attending, he exclaimed, "Oh, no. You have to be kidding! "

On arrival, JC noticed the car that belonged on one of his favorite volunteers. All excited, he raced into the house. But he stopped abruptly in the entertainment area when he saw six ladies seated at a table. He very formally went around the table smiling and shaking hands. He then repeated this with the men at the bar, before helping himself to crackers and dip, and settling down in a corner with his new Lego set.

Later, he was seen teaching a couple of interested ladies some sign language. He was the hit of the party and everyone kept saying what a bright, affectionate, curious boy he was. I have no idea how JC knew how to act in that new social situation; he'd certainly never been coached and had never previously been to an adult party.

As he approached adolescence, it became clear that JC had both the social skills to charm whomever he met and an independent streak that led him to leave home unannounced, maybe returning hours later or needing to be tracked down by worried staff, even days later, far from home.

JC first went missing when he was 11. During the August school holidays, he and María had moved to El Salto to share a house with her future husband and his son's family. The daughter-in-law was openly hostile to María and JC and he was so terrified of her that he ran away one Saturday morning in early September. María arrived at school on Monday, frantically worried. The search began. Teacher Citlali drove to Guadalajara to make a missing person report on local TV and radio. Meanwhile, Dr. Freeman King, a US consultant who had just arrived at the school, drove María, teacher Rita and me to El Salto seeking leads. It took us three afternoons to locate him, plus a stress-inducing night trip to the Guadalajara morgue to investigate a misidentified body.

JC had spent one night at a Catholic seminary, where a visiting psychologist, who knew some sign language, offered to drive him home. JC had declined the offer. After breakfast, they let him walk out the gate and did not notify any authorities.

Five days after he first went missing, we finally found him—14 kilometres from María's new home, playing in the sand in front of a house where a woman had kindly given him food and a bed for two nights. The rescue party was in tears and JC kept signing "*disculpe, disculpe,*" (I'm sorry, I'm sorry).

El Salto, JC's new home town, was 60 kilometres from Jocotepec, and not on a direct bus route. María was no longer a student at the school. To keep him safe and attending school, I had JC stay with me weekdays in my small house in Jocotepec. He learned to cook basic meals and loved studying illustrated cooking books. With a little guidance, he even baked a birthday cake for his mother.

He made friends with the neighbourhood boys by taking paper and pencils outdoors to do arithmetic with them, or inviting them into the house to look at picture books and his beloved *National Geographic* magazines. Some nights he carefully followed the illustrated instructions to build machines with his Lego, a gift sent by his first teacher, Susan van Gurp. He would show me newly added moving parts, excitedly signing "I know. I know. *Rápido.*"

María brought him to school on Monday mornings. On Fridays he travelled with teacher Rita and other deaf students back to Ixtlahuacán to meet María. But he kept leaving, without permission, even from my home. It was as if his early life, alone and independent, wandering the streets, still captivated him. In the 15 months following his first long disappearance, he left home nine times, to be brought back days later by staff or police from villages around the lake or Guadalajara. The loud speaker in the Jocotepec church was forever broadcasting that JC was missing again.

At age 13, during the school holidays, JC wandered off once more from El Salto after he signed to María that he didn't want (or need?) a mother now. This time, no search party went looking for him. Six months later, teacher Rita happened to see his photo on a TV program featuring unidentified and missing children. He was living happily over 500 kilometres away in a children's home in Mexico City, where staff took him daily to a special education school. María visited him every month or so. JC's social worker reported he was well behaved and helpful. She asked María for a copy of his birth certificate but she didn't have one.

Later, JC returned to live with María and her husband in their new house. A classic "street kid"—charming but functionally illiterate—he would still take off for days at a time but otherwise worked alongside his bricklayer stepfather whom he called *papá*.

After his return from Mexico City, JC's birth certificate was finally located. He had been registered at birth, by one of María's friends, not as Juan Carlos—as María had intended—but as Juan Francisco.

5

Home away from home: The boarding program

The Lakeside School's unique family-based boarding program began out of necessity. As the program grew, the model seemed to work for all involved, so we did not switch to the traditional, residential school accommodation commonly associated with schools for the deaf in Canada and the US.

Our boarding students, often over 50% of the student population, stayed with local families. Most arrived at the house on Monday after school and left for home on Friday. Host families received a monthly delivery of dried foods from DIF Jalisco and a small weekly stipend from the school committee. The total recompense was certainly far from generous, and it is doubtful whether boarding homes actually benefitted financially from the arrangement, but it was all the committee felt it could afford when covering the costs of 23–25 boarders from the late 1980s onwards. A few of the host families were almost as poor as the families of the children they were helping, whilst others were working class, or even middle class, by local standards. We tried to place children so that there was not a big discrepancy between their own home and the standard of living in their boarding home.

Most of the host families accepted two or more students, which meant we were able to keep siblings together, if the families wished, even when there were four in the family. Only a few students, such as Juan Luis, boarded with the families of fellow deaf students.

Doña Ramona, housemother for Pedro X., making tortillas

Most lived with local families who had an extra bed available or with grandmothers with empty bedrooms and big hearts.

Boarding students stayed with the same host family year after year, and the two families would usually become well acquainted with each other. Mothers or grandmothers boarding two or more deaf youngsters learned from them how to communicate in sign language, some quite well, all to at least a basic level. Some of the hearing children of those households attended our Saturday morning sign classes, eager to improve their communication with their deaf friends.

The first student to board in Jocotepec was María Elena, aged 5 on arrival in September 1983, who stayed with Jackie and Roma for two years, along with two other young Mexican children who lived with them. In August 1985 Roma was still in Canada recuperating from her injuries, so we needed to find Jocotepec families to care for María Elena and for Armando, a new student from her town, when school reopened in September. Teacher Citlali spoke with a group of women attending a class at the Jocotepec Development Centre and two immediately offered to board a child. Meanwhile, teacher Lola had found another family willing to accept boarding students. It seemed that finding host families was not going to be a major problem and, indeed, that remained true for the next decade, even as the boarding program expanded. It was teacher Lola who suggested that bulk food packages from DIF Jalisco, the social services agency, could be used as partial payment for the boarding homes. Her sister was the social worker at DIF Jocotepec.

New boarding students seemed to settle in with their new "families" within a few days, and were happy to return to the school and the boarding family the following Monday. It was often the students' parents who felt the separation most keenly during the school week, whilst the children were soon immersed in an exciting new world of communication and friendships. Indeed, they were brave parents who entrusted their young children to the care of an institution that was not well known, to live during the school week in a distant town with families who were not their relatives.

In a few unusual cases, the school, the committee and boarding family became entirely responsible for a child's welfare. The most extreme case was that of our autistic deaf student, Pedro X., with no known family, who was cared for by an amazing Jocotepec grandmother for 18 months.

Inevitably there were problems to solve with the boarding program. But most were not particularly serious: a student's complaint that the cooking at his boarding home was not the same as his mother's cooking; host families indicating that some batches of dried beans from DIF were of poor quality and so took twice as long to cook. Teacher Citlali occasionally organized a meeting of the ladies who cared for boarding students to talk about how best to work with deaf children and to discuss any concerns.

Food staples from DIF Jalisco

The food packages supplied by DIF Jalisco were certainly appreciated by the school as an important cost-saving contribution to the boarding program. However, we couldn't persuade DIF to make deliveries to Jocotepec, so someone had to drive to the Guadalajara warehouse each month to collect sacks of food. This was then repackaged by whichever former student was the school cook at the time, before being delivered to the boarding homes.

Each home received dried beans (*frijoles*), sugar, oil and powdered milk. It was good-tasting milk and the children all liked drinking it, especially with banana or cocoa whizzed in. Every Mexican home with electricity seemed to own a blender, so reconstituting the milk powder was never a problem. Sometimes we received a sack of flour. Since the local Mexican housewives used very little wheat flour, we traded it to a new Jocotepec *tortilleria* where they made wheat tortillas rather than the traditional corn version. They gave us the equivalent value in wheat tortillas, spread over the month. These made a nice change occasionally from corn tortillas for the school snack, topped with *frijoles*, chopped cabbage, *chile* and crumbled white cheese.

Much to our surprise, in March 1986, two days before the two week Easter vacation (Mexico's main public holiday), a DIF Jalisco truck arrived unexpectedly after school hours, and delivered fourteen 50-pound bags of powdered skimmed milk. What were we to do with 700 pounds of milk powder? Roma and I drove around next day to donate 50-pound bags of powdered milk to the primary school and the kindergartens in the nearby poor *barrio*, and to the Jocotepec Development Centre. It was good quality skimmed milk from the US. Local families were accustomed to reconstituting powdered milk as there was no bottled pasteurized milk on sale locally.

Then, three months later, at 6.00pm in the evening, a DIF truck arrived at Roma's house with our monthly food rations (which they would normally not deliver) and another 700 pounds of California non-fat dried milk. It was only nine days before the long school holidays began and we still had three sacks of milk stored from the March delivery, thinking we'd never get another such shipment. Roma and I hurriedly organized extra mice-proofed storage in the school kitchen and again delivered sacks of milk around the community, shipping some to the *Niños y Jovenes* (Children and Youth) children's home in the next town, San Juan Cosalá, and bonus amounts to the boarding homes. Each student left for vacation that year with backpacks bulging with plastic bags of powdered milk, along with their holiday homework folders.

On two other occasions, the DIF food ration included a huge block of aged, tasty American cheese, not the soft mild cheese that was sometimes included. The Mexican families definitely did not like that strong-tasting cheese, so our cook cut it into one-pound blocks which were sold to delighted Ajijic friends of the school at US prices. Tasty cheese was unobtainable locally so we could have sold a ton of it. With the cash, we purchased local Mexican cheese for the lunch program and the boarding houses, a much appreciated addition to their usual rations.

As a staff, we never really considered changing our home-based boarding system to a mini-version of a residential school with all boarding students living in the one building with care staff. I had once stayed in the residence of the Alberta School for the Deaf for several weeks, and three of our staff had likewise been hosted in the residence of the Indiana School for the Deaf (chapter 7), so we were certainly aware of the standard Canadian or US system for boarding out-of-area students. But Mexico was different. Local families were prepared to accept the deaf students into their homes as if they were part of their extended family, and many long-term friendships were formed as a result. Also, the total number of boarders, 27 at one point in time, was not so large that it outran the supply of welcoming homes.

As teacher Citlali wrote in 2019, reflecting back on the boarding program:

> The parents trusted the teachers at the school, who were always looking out for the boarding students and the families that gave them hospitality. These generous people, without knowing the families of the children, received them into their homes and always were there to help them, to offer them love, attention and care. Many of them, to this day, still keep in touch.

Citlali had noted in 1989, after five years at the school, that "the local community has become more aware of the problems facing the deaf child, and more accepting of them in social situations."

The family-based boarding model almost certainly helped to form positive impressions of the deaf youngsters and their school in the community at large. The model also meant that the deaf students were not living in a restricted environment with only their deaf peers as companions. Rather, the home-based boarding program, by its very nature, encouraged the deaf children and teenagers to learn to communicate with people other than their own family, by using whatever speech they had mastered, and by teaching others their language of signs.

6

Individual stories: New students, 1984–1989

Here are the stories of some of the students who enrolled after the boarding program began.

Ilia

In early September 1985 a Huichol Indian girl, aged maybe 20, arrived at the school. She was staying with a local *doctora* (female doctor) who didn't know the girl's name. A priest from a Franciscan mission in the mountains of neighbouring Nayarit state had sent the girl from her tiny village to Jocotepec after meeting the *doctora*. Even though the young lady was very profoundly deaf, the priest wanted her to learn to talk!

During her third week at school, we were handing around a Bon Voyage card from class to class for students to sign because teacher Citlali was flying to Toronto for professional development. Suddenly the card went missing in the classroom of the newest students. Over the past few days they'd been learning language related to location. As we searched, Ilia began laughing and signing, *"Busca, busca"* (Search, search). She had hidden the card and was having a wonderful time, laughing and laughing as she controlled the classroom, answering "No, No", as fellow students questioned her. "Is it inside that box? Is it behind those books?" Finally, after many questions we got a "Yes" and the card was located.

Ilia was such a bright young lady, with a wonderful sense of humour, and it was really unfortunate that she did not return after the Christmas holidays.

Ivonne

Ivonne arrived at the school immediately following the September 1985 massive earthquake in Mexico City which killed at least 10,000 people and left some 50,000 families homeless. Ivonne's home and school had both collapsed in the quake. Ivonne and her mother fled to Jocotepec to stay for a long while with relatives after learning of the specialist school here. The earthquake was felt in Jocotepec, but our school building suffered only a few minor cracks. Ivonne, aged 10, with a severe hearing loss and hearing aids, had attended a regular school and then a school for the deaf for a few years. She knew basic Mexican sign language, could lip read and speak a little, but had virtually no written vocabulary. Her math was at about the same level as 8-year-old María Elena, who was really happy to have another girl in her class. Ivonne's mother and her Jocotepec relatives requested help in learning sign language, so I restarted the Saturday morning sign classes.

César and his family

Three of the four handsome children in this family—César, Miguel and Mirna— were deaf and attended the Lakeside School from April 1986 as boarders. The family lived on their farm near a tiny, isolated village in the Zacoalco municipality. The children had to take three busses to make the 50-kilometre trip to Jocotepec. Their father paid all the bus fares each week for the three children and an adult, who accompanied them to help flag down the intercity busses on the highway.

César was 15 when he arrived at the Lakeside School. He had sat for eight years in the village school where he had managed to figure out long multiplication and long division in math classes, but, like all our profoundly deaf students, he had not learned to read even the simplest sentences while attending overcrowded local schools. He struggled to write single words like "man, house, happy." Given small-group instruction, specialized teaching methods, sign language, amplified speech, and his sharp mind, César learned quickly and two years later could read basic Spanish.

César was a fine "big brother", not only to his younger siblings Miguel and Mirna, but to all the young boys at the school, especially the little ones who were boarding away from home. You had only to see the 4- and 5-year-olds run up to hug him round the legs on Monday morning to know who was teaching them to kick a soccer ball at recess and who gave them a ride home on his shoulders in the mid-afternoon heat. César willingly worked around the school after hours with older student José, helping with maintenance and gardening without expecting pay as he understood the school and his American sponsor were covering the cost of his education and lodging.

In 1993, after six years as a boarding student, César was employed full-time at the school in charge of maintenance and the grounds, a position he still holds in 2019. He also teaches some woodworking classes each week. César married a fellow student, Lorena, and their severely deaf children have been successfully integrated into local schools with some support from specialist teachers and former teachers of the Lakeside School.

Bety

A sweet-natured little girl from Jocotepec, Bety started school in October 1986 as a 3-year-old with no idea of even basic communication, like waving goodbye. No matter what happened, Bety just smiled. Her young mother, with four children under 6, had provided little or no cognitive or language stimulation for her profoundly deaf daughter.

It was several months before Bety used her first expressive signs. Then, at the 1986 Christmas concert, before an audience of over 100, Bety and 4-year-old Paty presented a dance number that brought the house down and moistened a lot of Kleenex. Her young mother was crying with pride and joy. After that, Bety, once almost totally ignored by her family, began to communicate as her mother took a new interest in her and started to learn some sign language. Over time, Bety developed into a charming and very lovable little girl, the fixed smile replaced by a range of emotions. She needed lots of one-to-one help in class and her progress with language and arithmetic seemed sometimes to be affected by problems at home. It took Bety a little longer than others to grasp new concepts like "same/different" but she was always willing to try again and was proud of her successes. After 18 months at school, Bety was attempting to tell about her daily life and starting to understand questions addressed to her. Students and teachers treated her with affection, encouraging her to communicate with signs, voice and lots of hugs.

In 1988, when her mother moved the family out of town, Bety began living with her kindergarten teacher, Rita. By then, Bety's mother was convinced that the little girl *could* learn and should continue to attend the Lakeside School, which she did for the next three years until her mother moved all the family again, this time to California.

Socorro H.

Socorro H. lived in Santa Cruz de las Flores, 45 kilometres from Jocotepec. Her oldest brother, a bus driver, was assigned to the Chapala–Jocotepec route and had regularly transported some of our students and staff to and from school for two years. In October 1987 he finally plucked up the nerve to tell one of the teachers that he had a young "cousin"— who turned out to be his 9-year-old sister—who was deaf and had never been to school.

Asked why he had waited so long to let us know this, he said, *"Me dio vergüenza"* ("I was ashamed").

Socorro turned out to be a sweet, independent, highly intelligent and industrious girl, certainly not someone to be ashamed of. Her family agreed to let her board Monday to Friday with teacher Rita and her deaf son. When she started, Socorro could copy letters but couldn't read a single word except for her name. It is doubtful we ever had another student who grasped written language faster than Socorro. Within six weeks she could read and act out her first simple sentences, and read and sign the colours, the days of the week and much more. Socorro was obviously delighted to be at school and it was such a pity that she attended for only two years.

Mario M.

Mario M., pictured on the front cover, lived in María Elena's town of Arenal near Tequila, and enrolled in November 1986. I had driven to Arenal and met the young mother of 4-year-old Mario and his two siblings in their one-room, dirt-floor home by the railway line. Although she had only a year or two of schooling herself, and her young husband was illiterate, she wanted Mario to have an education and agreed he could start school as a boarder the following Monday.

Mother and son did indeed arrive as promised, accompanied by María Elena and a family member. For the next eight years, Mario would board four nights a week with Sra. Evelia's family who already cared for María Elena. On arrival, Mario was small for his age, very light weight and was pronounced mal-nourished by our local nurse. His health improved once at school as he was well fed in his Jocotepec boarding home, enjoyed nutritious food at morning recess at school, and later became active in the sports and horticulture programs.

Mario started school one week after his 4th birthday. Within days he began signing expressively, a rare achievement. Mario was

Teacher Nena instructing on care of pets, 1988. Standing (L-R) Mirna (César's sister), Socorro H., Carlos. Seated: Pablo, Juan Luis, León

a great little communicator who added pantomime and expressive gestures to his formal sign language so that all could understand him. Mario was such a good-looking, cute little guy, with such an engaging affectionate personality, that he was much photographed by visitors, many of whom wanted to take him home with them. A few years later he was selected to be the star of the school's publicity video.

Mario had Waardenburg syndrome, a rare genetic disorder that caused his profound deafness and also resulted in him having one blue eye and one brown eye. In his kinder class, a year after his arrival, the children were learning to name facial features and were each given a mirror so they could try drawing self-portraits. Mario, then aged 5, was extremely surprised to discover he had one brown eye and one blue eye. For the next few days, he excitedly told everybody he met about this.

Throughout his eight years at the school, Mario always had a positive attitude about learning to read, write and speak basic Spanish, and made regular progress academically. He was an enthusiastic participant in many extracurricular activities and continued to brighten everyone's day with his humour and his infectious smiles. Then, in December 1994, tragedy struck. Mario was at home for the Christmas holidays. He asked his mother for a few pesos to buy a yogurt for breakfast from the little store across the railroad tracks. We don't know exactly how it happened, but Mario was hit and killed by a passing train. All the staff attended the funeral in Arenal. He was mourned and deeply missed by all who had known and loved him.

Juan Luis

One Sunday in September 1987 a truck driver pulled up at teacher Rita's house in Ixtlahuacán de los Membrillos, looking for the teacher of the deaf. Down climbed a thin, good-looking young boy, clutching his bag of clothes. The driver had promised to drop off "Carlos" as a favour to the boy's aunt who lived outside Guadalajara, saying he'd been told the boy needed to get a hearing aid. Carlos held up six fingers to indicate his age. Rita put up a camp bed, accepted him into the family as companion to her own deaf 9-year-old son, and brought him to school on Monday. We had had no prior notice of our new student.

The next Sunday, an aunt arrived at Rita's and exclaimed, "Oh, no. His name is not Carlos. It's Juan Luis." And he was nearly nine years old... a 9-year-old who simply didn't know his own name. It seems his mother had abandoned him at some point in the past, and his next caregiver used to send him out into the streets of Guadalajara to beg. He was rescued by his aunt, but she had a large family of her own and could not get the little boy to and from the distant state school for the deaf in the centre of the city.

At school the next day, we erased the name "Carlos" from his note books and created a different sign name for him. Juan Luis had obviously never been to kinder or primary school. He painstakingly

learned to print letters and copy his name, and initially wrestled
with number concepts from 1 to 5. However, he was a bright youngster who learned fast; nothing in his new environment daunted
him. He had loads of personality and spunk and was a great little
ham and a truly lovable kid. With sign language and a hearing aid
(which he liked to wear) he soon became quite a "chatterbox." For
the first time in his life he was able to communicate with friends,
ask questions, and learn what was happening or going to happen.

His relatives showed little interest in him and months would
pass with no contact from the family. The Lakeside School,
through the sponsor program, covered all his costs, including
boarding, clothing, medical bills, school supplies and transport.
Juan Luis continued to live with Rita and her family, celebrating
with large family fiestas, milestones like his First Communion,
along with Rita's own deaf son, Juan Diego. (chapter 7)

At age 15, Juan Luis was still attending classes till 1.30 each
day. Then, in the afternoons and on Saturdays, he had a work
experience placement in Ixtlahuacán de los Membrillos. Thanks
to teacher Elizabeth, Juan Luis was learning to design, shape and
solder wrought iron furniture in her husband's workshop.

Brothers Israel and Alejandro

The family of Israel, 5, and Alejandro, nearly 3, decided to move
out of the busy city of Guadalajara and chose the small town
of Jocotepec because of the reputation of the Lakeside School.
Alejandro had attended the large, overcrowded, government kindergarten for the deaf in Guadalajara for a few hours daily for six
months and Israel had attended for a year or so. They started at
the 29-student Lakeside School in March 1988 after staff found
the family a house to rent. Their father was a travelling salesman.
His wife—well-educated and the mother of three—killed and
dressed a few chickens from her tiny backyard pen each morning
to sell from a table in front of the house to help make ends meet.

In June 1988 we celebrated the 3rd birthday of Alejandro, our youngest student. He was a little confused about the cake and candles and the Mexican birthday song, but enjoyed receiving his small present, and a hug and greetings (*"Felicidades"*, signed and spoken) from each student.

Israel and Alejandro were both handsome, bright, severely deaf little boys with unusual "ski-slope" audiograms. Once fitted with donated hearing aids and using FM amplifiers in class, they heard some of the sounds of speech almost normally, but not the important high frequency speech sounds where their loss was profound. Small class sizes and the use of sign language along with speech allowed them to develop age-appropriate vocabulary and concepts in the kinder years. Teachers insisted that the boys always used speech or approximated the pronunciation of words.

By May 1992 we were in discussion with the boys' parents about integrating them into a regular primary school in September. After four years at the Lakeside School, their math and reading skills would allow them to succeed in Grades 1 and 2 and both boys could, by then, manage orally in a controlled situation. For the next two years, teacher Elizabeth provided speech and language tutorials each morning from 8.30–10.00am for Israel, Alejandro and three other integrated students, who then attended the afternoon session of primary school from 2.00–6.30pm. Alejandro and Israel continued to participate in special events for the Lakeside School, like the Christmas concerts of 1992 and '93 and the annual Jalisco Olympics for the Deaf where the brothers always won gold. Both boys successfully completed regular Grade 6 without having to repeat any year.

By their late 20s, both Israel and Alejandro were financially stable, happily married, bringing up hearing children, and each was running a small business. Alejandro had his own auto body repair and painting workshop and Israel had started a business replacing and polarizing car windscreens. Amazingly, given their severe hearing loss, both young men have developed normal-sounding speech, and conversation flows naturally when talking with them. Their parents' decision to move the family to Jocotepec to be near the Lakeside School when the boys were very young had certainly had a positive outcome.

Pedro X., a very special kid

No one knows his real name, age or address. Police found the profoundly deaf 7- or 8-year-old living on the streets of Guadalajara and placed him in a children's home. He had third degree malnutrition and exhibited some autistic-like self-destructive behaviours. After six months no one had claimed him. He was brought to the Lakeside School in January 1988, barefoot, his worldly possessions the shirt and jeans he was wearing. He had few social skills and no means of communication.

After a month at school, Pedro was much calmer and able to work with the kindergarten class for short periods before he needed time in his own private world, whirling his sticks and wheels in the garden. Margaret Green, a volunteer assistant experienced with special needs children, frequently worked with Pedro, helping him to relate to people and adjust to the school routine. By the end of the '88 school year, Pedro could work for an entire lesson beside the junior kinder children, tracing his name, arranging shapes and painting. He was no longer hurting himself, was becoming quite affectionate with staff and sometimes even ran out to greet visitors. However, he did not start using any sign language himself, and only responded to a few basic signs like "food, water, sleep."

Thankfully, an elderly Mexican couple were prepared to provide a home for Pedro during the school year. He obviously loved "grandmother" Doña Ramona, who cared for him at much cost to her own peace of mind and freedom of movement as he required constant vigilance and a locked front door.

One day, a volunteer drove Pedro to Guadalajara for assessment by medical specialists at the Dr. Ángel Leaño Hospital. Pedro's profound hearing loss was confirmed. Then a neurologist spent a few minutes with him and declared that since he could not communicate with him, there was no chance of him learning anything. However, as if to prove him wrong, Pedro then displayed some advanced visual-directional skills. Shown the car keys, he quickly led the way out of that large hospital, not even re-tracing the route they'd taken to get to the various offices. Once outside he made a bee line across the huge parking lot, locating the car without a moment's hesitation.

Pedro was included in our major school excursions. On a trip to the Guadalajara zoo, he wandered away while staff were setting out the picnic lunch. Frantic searching soon located him, cooling off under a fountain, stark naked. On the three-day excursion to the Pacific, several male volunteers kept him under surveillance at all times. He would stand for ages, gazing into the water, "stimming" on the shallow waves breaking around his feet, at peace in a world of his own.

At the end of the 1989 school year we reluctantly placed Pedro in an enclosed Guadalajara children's home. Although he had made real improvement in his behaviour and his ability to relate to other people, he was not learning any language skills. He still needed constant supervision if he were not to break our equipment (like the video player) or take-off jogging down the centre of the nearest highway, focused only on the white line.

7

Inspiring Teachers

A single lighthouse
opens hearts and minds
on Lake Chapala.

Fingers and hands flash
an ancient system
mind is transformed.

- Poem, dedicated to the teachers, by J. Freeman King

It can't be stressed enough that in educational circles teaching severely and profoundly deaf students is considered one of the most difficult roles in special education. Given the atypical background of most of our students and the teachers' initial lack of specialist preparation, the challenge for our teachers was even greater than usual.

What motivated teachers to take on the challenge of such a different role and then to continue teaching at the school?

Primarily, it was the opportunity to make a really huge difference in some young lives. It was the knowledge that the skills you taught daily in your classroom—by sign language, speech, reading, writing and creative activities—offered these children and teenagers their only real chance to learn how to communicate effectively with others, to learn of the world outside their homes, to master life skills and gain vocational training. When a 9-year-old child arrives at school and cannot write his own name, nor speak it, nor recognize it in speech or print, you realize his world has failed him miserably. But you also know that you and your colleagues and the other students can transform his world and help him to become a young man who is proud of who he is and what he can do.

Secondly, the "one big family" atmosphere, which we deliberately fostered at the school, helped keep morale high amongst staff, volunteers and the students, too. Teachers generally felt involved in the welfare and education of all the students, not just the six or so in their classroom that year. There was more than the usual willingness to share teaching strategies and materials, to suggest local resources, to jointly celebrate milestones and achievements in any of the students' lives, and to actively help solve any student or school crisis.

"Dedicated" was the word most often used to describe our staff by visitors, experts and the local press. Visitors would quickly sense that the teachers were indeed heavily invested in improving the lives of their students by their planning, creativity and individual focus in the classroom.

One visitor to our three-day Open House in January 1988 was Mildred Dovey, a recently retired teacher of the deaf and program administrator from Pennsylvania. In an article about the school in the *Pittsburgh Press* she later wrote, "The thing that struck me right away at the school was the dedication of the teachers and how little of the material things they had to work with. They have to improvise; they can't pick up a McGraw-Hill catalogue and order what they need."

After his visit in 1990, Mr David Winfield, the Canadian Ambassador to Mexico, praised, "the obvious work and care which all concerned devote to the school and students.... One has a very strong sense that the students genuinely feel loved and cared for, a key to encouraging personal growth and learning."

The staff was also willing, as a group, to commit the time and energy to extracurricular projects that sometimes seemed to me far too ambitious for our small team to tackle. But the teachers, with help from some committee volunteers, would enthusiastically plan events that became the highlights of our students' school years. So, for example, we produced elaborate Christmas concerts every year, took the whole school on a three-day excursion to the Pacific, and hosted and organized a two-day Olympic Games for over 300 deaf student competitors from around the state. (chapter 10)

There was an additional reason why our staffing remained fairly stable from the late 1980s on. The teachers who had taught in government schools appreciated the freedom from the onerous amount of paper work and red tape, the hierarchy and top-down decision-making that characterized the public education system at the time.

However, employment at the school had major financial disincentives. It meant surviving on a near-subsistence salary (roughly equal to the take-home pay of the lowest rung of the public school teachers' pay scale), with no adequate medical plan, no pension plan, and no access to the low-interest housing loans available through the government. Thankfully, our all-female staff either had husbands who were the main family breadwinners or, if single, lived in the family home as was traditional in rural Mexico. Teachers in Mexico almost always held down two jobs, teaching at one school in the morning and another in the afternoon or evening, because they could not support a family on one teaching salary.

Teacher training programs in Mexico in the 1980s

Programs for teacher training varied widely and the background of our teachers on arrival at the school reflected this.

Some, like teachers Citlali Bravo and Elizabeth Monge, had completed four-year training courses plus some years of classroom teaching experience. Citlali was a well-qualified Kindergarten-

Grade 1 teacher with teaching experience. Elizabeth had a degree in Special Education and two years experience in the state of Sonora, teaching deaf children in an oral program.

Others, like teachers Lupita Olmedo and Linda Reyes, held the standard two-year teacher training certificate and had taught for at least two years in regular primary schools before switching to the Lakeside School and a very different teaching experience. Whilst employed at the school in the 1990s, teachers Lupita, Linda, Gaby and Josefina began 5 years of part-time study in Guadalajara to eventually earn their Bachelors Degree in Special Education, specializing in Audition and Language.

Teacher Gaby Escamilla had originally begun her teaching career with a bursary in the mid-1980s without completing senior high school, in a system called rural teacher or community instructor. After a brief introductory course, she taught Grades K–6 in a one-room school in a tiny, isolated community. She returned to Guadalajara for intensive courses during every school holiday for two years before eventually taking full-time courses. The *rancho* where she lived and taught had no electricity or piped water, nor even toilets until several fathers there built an outdoor toilet for Gaby. Gaby and the women walked a kilometre to get water and to wash clothes. The impoverished families in such *ranchos* rotated the provision of basic accommodation and meals for the teacher under an agreement with the education department, in order to have a teacher in their tiny outlying settlements.

How did we find our teachers?

From around 1988 onwards, the school employed five to seven classroom teachers who formed a fairly stable staff for the next six years. Visitors, especially those with a teaching background, would often ask in amazement, "Where did you find these teachers?" for it was clear we had a core of teachers with exceptional natural teaching ability, creativity and total commitment to the

(L-R) Lupita, Citlali, Veronica, Nena, Gwen. Above, question words with visual cues for students

education of their students, in the widest sense. Former education administrators, who came to know the staff well over the course of several years, expressed their admiration for this extraordinary group of teachers, both as individuals and as a team.

In most cases, our teachers heard of the school through friends and family and, upon investigating, found the vocation they were looking for. Teacher Citlali's relative, Sylvia Flores, founder of the Jocotepec (Women's) Development Centre, came to the school in 1984 to inquire whether we needed a great kindergarten teacher. Citlali had just married and moved to her husband's home town of Jocotepec. Teacher Elizabeth's husband came to see if we might need a specialist teacher of the deaf in 1990, having just moved his new bride from her home state of Sonora, northern Mexico, to his home town near Chapala. In teacher Gaby's case, it was her younger, severely deaf brother, a student at the Lakeside School, who linked her to the school. Teachers Lupita, Linda, and Nena Garibay heard of the school's need for teachers from friends already working at the school or at the Women's Development Centre.

For the first eight or nine years of the school's existence, however, trying to find suitable teachers, finding the means to train them in the specialty, and then finding they needed to leave for family reasons, sometimes proved to be disappointing and frustrating experiences.

In early 1984, as Susan and I contemplated returning to Canada at the end of our second year at Lakeside, we advertised widely in US and Canada for a specialist replacement, there being no one available locally. Only one recently graduated American teacher of the deaf finally committed to coming. Ida M. was bilingual and of Mexican-American descent. Perfect, we thought. Susan flew back to Canada and I agreed to stay for a few months to help with the transition. Ida arrived in Jocotepec in mid-August, before the start of the school year, suffered some type of extreme culture shock and left before she even met the students!

Miraculously, teachers Citlali Bravo and Sara Ortega had arrived in town about then and both decided to take up the challenge of in-service training, joining teacher Lola and me as the school year began that September. Teacher Lola resigned in December 1985, expecting her second child, after five years of loyal and caring service to the school's earliest students. As the first teacher hired by Jackie and Roma in early 1980, she had been the only Mexican—and the only native Spanish speaker—on staff until Citlali and Sara began teaching in 1984.

Sara had been a teacher for many years, most recently teaching English and Spanish as a Second Language. In 1986 she devoted countless hours to translating a detailed US curriculum for the deaf into Spanish for our immediate and future use. Unfortunately, Sara was never sure how long she could stay and had to resign in December 1986 due to family commitments in Guadalajara. Her class of seniors and young adults declared they had "learnt a lot" from teacher Sara's lively classroom presentations.

Meanwhile, Irma, a young teacher with certification as a kindergarten teacher, joined the staff in September 1986 and had classroom in-service training with our US consultant Dr. Freeman King for several months. Sixteen months later, she failed to return to teach her class after Christmas. We learned she had eloped over the holidays and she never reappeared at the school.

In 1987, with a growing student population, local advertising for teachers proved as unsuccessful as our previous international search in 1984. We would be visited by applicants with no teaching background whatsoever, such as a French-speaking young lady, a Mexican computer technician, and others who never returned after viewing classes and learning of the low salary. One applicant, a family man with deaf parents, said he could sign well... said he was sure he could learn to be a teacher. However, we didn't offer him a position when we found he only had Grade 6 education.

Then, in September 1987, we thought we would finally have a male staff member when an experienced senior high school teacher started in-service training. But he didn't naturally "connect" with the students and found the intense focus needed by teachers in the classroom to be exhausting. He kept telling us at recess what a "tough job this is" and resigned after six weeks, just as we'd decided to tell him *"Adiós."*

Thus, six teachers left between June 1984 and December 1987: Susan to Canada (June 1984), Ida to the US (August 1984), Lola to motherhood (December 1985), Sara to family (December 1986), male teacher quit (October 1987) and Irma eloped (December 1987).

Thankfully, as noted, our staffing stabilized after that. In all my years at the school, there was only one teacher whose contract we did not renew after a year. She was an experienced teacher from Mexico City, who seemed unprepared to match the team work, the commitment to the children, and the energy of the rest of the staff.

In-service teacher training at the Lakeside School

Susan van Gurp and I organized our classes and teaching methods based on our understanding, from Canadian schools, of best practice

Citlali's kindergarten class learn about the radio in a communications theme

in the teaching of profoundly deaf students. However, given that we were mainly working with older students with little or no educational background, and given the lack of commercial educational materials, adaptation was a constant, every lesson, for every student.

As each new teacher arrived, in-service training consisted initially of classroom observation whilst they learned to communicate with sign language, with theory taught after class. After teacher Sara joined us in mid-1984, she and I spent many evenings each week for several months covering teaching methodology, sign language and basic audiology, while she taught a class of newly-enrolled senior students each morning. When teacher Nena started, she had six months in-service before taking over her own class. Sometimes though, in-service for experienced primary school teachers was considerably shorter when a class needed a teacher due to circumstances like a staff member leaving or going on maternity leave.

As teachers gained more experience and specialized knowledge, in-service of new staff became more of a cooperative endeavour. This was particularly true of Citlali's role, as she supervised the progress of new teachers working with kindergarten and early primary classes.

Citali's own professional development included specialist training from several outside agencies. Citlali had always wanted to work in special education but had not had the opportunity to do so until she started teaching at the Lakeside School. Citlali offered her services as a volunteer in October 1984 whilst she learned sign language and the special teaching methods.

She recalls thinking during her first week at the school that she would never be able to work with the deaf—the teaching techniques were so different to those used with regular students. In addition, it was difficult to get accustomed to the strange sounds made by new students who had not learned to control their voices. But the family atmosphere at the small school and the chance to learn about deaf education convinced her to stay. In January 1985 she took charge of a class when I returned to Canada.

Citlali is bilingual and so was selected in the fall of 1985, after I returned to the Lakeside, to spend six weeks in Toronto observing at the Toronto School for the Deaf and learning about practical audiology at a hospital audiology clinic. That experience was organized by Gordon Kerr and sponsored by the Canadian International Hearing Services (CIHS) and a Toronto Rotary Club. The following year Citlali participated in the in-service training for staff at the school, provided by Professor Freeman King.

Citlali recognized that the school was in the vanguard of special education for the deaf in Mexico—not only in terms of materials but also in its educational programs. She believed the school could become a model for other Mexican schools to follow if we could provide still more training for our teachers and strengthen our finances.[7]

From September through December 1988, whilst I was on maternity leave, Citlali was the acting director. New teacher Gaby, who could already sign, team taught with Citlali during her in-service training. This gave Citlali time to attend to visitors, audiology needs, and the endless emergencies. She was responsible for the programming for the Christmas concert that year and also organized a linguistics course for all staff.

In April 1990 Citlali was one of three staff who spent two weeks as guests at the Indiana School for the Deaf and who later shared their experiences and insights with all our staff.

In-service training with US consultant

From September to mid-November 1986, we were fortunate to have a visiting consultant: Professor Freeman King, Director of Teacher Education for the Deaf at Lamar University, Beaumont, Texas.

Dr. King elected to spend part of his sabbatical year at our school, inspired by an earlier visit in 1984. He offered guidance in specialized teaching techniques and brought with him a detailed skills-based curriculum for the deaf. Our staff participated enthusiastically, staying after school almost every day for workshops. Anita Bish and teacher Sarah Ortega translated the materials for us. We later made this curriculum—almost certainly the first ever curriculum for the deaf available in Spanish in Mexico—available to other schools. Dr. King also provided in-service training in the classroom for our newest teacher, Irma. On a later visit, in April 1987, Dr. King, with the assistance of the adult deaf community in Guadalajara, produced video tapes teaching Mexican sign language, for use by parents and new staff.

The school newsletter later thanked him for "his valuable and lively involvement with our staff and for enchanting our students."[8] It also expressed thanks to Jane Osburn for providing Dr. King with free accommodation in her garden *casita* in Ajijic and stressed that Dr. King's work came at no cost to the committee.

Conference for teachers

In May 1987 the Lakeside School hosted a five-day conference for 45 teachers and language therapists, 38 of them from Guadalajara schools for the deaf and from DIF Guadalajara. Dr. King had obtained funding and recruited four professors from two Texas universities who presented a wealth of ideas and fielded questions. Unfortunately, sweltering May weather on the last two days was too much for our two new ceiling fans and we were like roast chickens in the old chicken coop. The conference would not have been possible without the volunteer assistance for the whole week of our amazing translator, local journalist Dale Hoyt Palfrey. Following the conference, a useful exchange of materials and services was established between the Guadalajara schools and our school.

Spanish grammar course

In early August 1988 teacher Citlali organized an excellent, intensive, five-day course in grammar-syntax-linguistics just for our staff at the school, presented by a lecturer from the Guadalajara Teachers' College. (Such content is a core element in teacher training courses in deaf education in the US and Canada.) This study of Spanish language structure was much needed by all of us and we refined our language curriculum as a result of the course. As I wrote to Susan van Gurp in Canada:

> This staff is really a conscientious group and it was then their idea to keep meeting one or two days a week for the rest of the holidays to fine tune the Social Science and Science curriculums pre-K to Grade 6. Our content and methods bear little resemblance to the outdated Mexican national curriculum.

Staff professional development with the Jocotepec Development Centre

Several of our teachers—Lupita, Citlali, Gaby and Nena—were also part-time members of the team that assisted registered nurse Sylvia Flores at the Jocotepec Development Centre, an outreach program to local villages that focused on education about female health issues, including birth control. The centre was a non-profit program begun in 1982, the year Susan and I started teaching at the Lakeside School. Both projects began without financial resources and both successfully sought national and international funding from foundations, some of which enabled Sylvia's clinic to offer professional development to her staff.

One such venture included two of our teachers, Lupita and Gaby, attending a three-week course in Mexico City on Adolescence while I taught their combined classes. Another time, all our teachers attended an intensive workshop for four afternoons on values education and sex education for teenagers given at the Jocotepec Development Centre by professionals from Mexico City. The course was rated excellent by our teachers. They were thus well qualified to teach the topic to our teenagers and held classes at Sylvia's clinic, using the Centre's videos and other visual materials, in very practical presentations, including family planning, that our teenagers really appreciated.

Audiology workshops

All staff attended a very informative week-long audiology workshop in August 1989, sponsored by the Canadian International Hearing Services and presented by Canadian audiologist Glen Sutherland. Glen returned in September 1992 to present a further intense two-day workshop, again sponsored by CIHS. (chapter 11)

Staff visit to Indiana School for the Deaf

In April 1990 teachers Citlali and Lupita and teaching assistant Veronica, spent two weeks at the 680-student Indiana School for the Deaf. Board and lodging were provided by the US school and travel costs were covered by Mrs. Binkie Chater and three other Lakeside residents. The idea for this trip arose after a group of senior students from the Indiana School had been guests at the Lakeside School the previous year.

The two week visit was voted an unqualified success, not only by the participants, but also by the rest of the staff. Our teachers were accommodated in the guest suite in the student residence and were thus able to experience all facets of life and learning at the huge school. Thanks to the friendliness and helpfulness of all the staff at the Indiana School, they returned with a great fund of ideas on curriculum methods and materials, which they shared with the Lakeside School staff in over a dozen workshops. They were amazed at the amount and variety of commercial teaching aids available to the Indiana staff (which unfortunately are not produced in Spanish). Despite this, they found that our teaching methods, using teacher-made materials, were not greatly different to those of the US. They did, however, stress the need for more emphasis on reading and presented several sessions demonstrating some methods of teaching reading at different levels which they had observed.

One problem our reading program faced, as Jackie Hartley had realized years earlier, was the almost total lack of interesting easy-to-read children's books in Spanish (high interest/low vocabulary) such as were readily available for special education in English north of the border. Each year I would spend a Saturday at the huge Guadalajara International Book Fair searching in vain for such books.

International experts provide training

In March 1992 three teachers—Linda, Gaby and Josefina—attended a very informative three-day workshop on teaching speech to the deaf by the international authority in the field, Dr. Daniel Ling of Canada. The course was held in the neighbouring state of San Luis Potosí and our participation was funded by the YMCA of Alberta, Canada.

In August 1992 teachers Lupita and Aby, accompanied by three parents of kindergarten children, participated in a five-day parent education seminar presented by staff of the world famous John Tracy Clinic of Los Angeles whose Spanish language course for parents was used in our program. This course was also held in San Luis Potosí and individual Lakeside donors helped cover our costs.

Beyond the call of duty

For most of our teachers over the years, their commitment to their students did not end at the school gate nor was it limited to the years the students were attending the school. Favorite teachers are often guests at milestone celebrations of former students. Former staff will still provide sign language translation when needed, for example in assisting a young adult to obtain a driving license, and still offer friendship and counselling to former students who arrive at their doorsteps. The following are just a few examples of "after hours" teacher involvement in the 1980s and 90s.

During Juan Carlos' first year at school (chapter 4), teacher Citlali and her husband would sometimes have the young boy stay with them for the weekend, introducing him to a different lifestyle and teaching him things boys need to learn from their fathers. One weekend they took him to visit the colonial city of Morelia in the next state for a day at the Morelia zoo. Juan Carlos was so enraptured by the animals that he cried when they had to leave.

Afternoons, after school hours, often found teachers volunteering time to help with various projects. Teacher Sara supervised Juan Carlos' mother, María, as she learned to sew curtains for their one-room home using a school sewing machine. Teacher Lupita would volunteer to attend afternoon meetings in Guadalajara, representing the school, so that our students could participate in inter-school events like the annual Olympic Games and student camps.

Teachers Linda, Nena and others from the town were, of course, more attuned to the local culture than I was, and had personal and family links with local officials, merchants, staff at government schools, and professionals who could help us with services, information, assistance with student events and local excursions. Without cars or telephones, making contacts and organizing help often entailed much after-school time by the teachers, always with the aim of enhancing the students' educational or vocational experiences.

For several years the teachers took voluntary English classes on Saturday mornings, first in Ajijic with Margaret Green, then with Betty and Robert Vázquez, and later with Robert Carter, so that they could better communicate with our many visitors.

Robert Carter was a former school administrator from Texas. When he learned that teacher Lupita was an excellent folkloric dancer, he invited her to Midland, Texas, to seek funds for the school. Lupita danced at several schools in the city in October 1990 and presented songs in sign language in various churches. As well as the donations for the school received at each event, the Bishop of San Ángelo made a personal donation of $1500.

When 13-year-olds Juan Diego, son of former teacher Rita, and Juan Luis, her full-time boarding student, jointly celebrated their First Communion in Ixtlahuacán one Sunday, 24 fellow students and two teachers, Gaby and Elizabeth attended the ceremony. Juan Diego's local American godmother, who had covered the cost of these celebrations, later wrote to the *Chapala Riviera Guide* that:

> The entire service was signed by the teachers who stood next to the priest. The hymns were also signed, and the students "sang" along with the choir.... Afterwards at the reception, along with music, "singing" and dancing, there were speeches and toasts, all interpreted with signing. All the Lakeside Deaf School children were beautifully behaved, happy, healthy and bright with excitement. The school is to be commended for the splendid job they are doing with these youngsters.[9]

Decades after the students left the school, former staff are still invited guests to special ceremonies like the graduation celebration in 2019 for Arturo's Bachelor of Fine Arts (chapter 9), and the wedding of two former students in 2018. At both events, as with many over the years, teachers offered to provide signed translation of the ceremonies for the celebrant and their deaf friends.

The teachers' career paths

The teachers who, by 1988, formed such an admired staff have since moved onwards and upwards in educational circles. Teachers Linda and Lupita are both directors of Special Education Centres in the region. Teacher Gaby earned her Masters in Special Education, continues to teach at the Lakeside school in the morning and provides assistance to integrated special education students in the afternoon. Teacher Elizabeth also works with integrated special needs students and their teachers. For many years Citlali operated her own private afternoon tutorial centre for students needing extra help with speech, language and literacy development. After I returned to Canada in 1997, she was also employed by the school committee, two mornings a week for some 14 years, to continue the hearing aid program for local students.

A Mexican teacher's viewpoint

Citlali, who was the Lakeside School's vice-principal, included the following in a memoir of her years teaching at the school—her point-of-view is shared by many who taught alongside her:

I will always appreciate having had the chance to be part of this educational project, which gave me the opportunity to develop as a teacher and the good fortune to have met such capable, marvellous and generous people—teachers, volunteers, audiologists and parents. I am especially grateful to my teacher and friend Gwen Chan who has always shared her knowledge with me and been a great help in furthering my training as a teacher of the deaf and as an audiology technician.

I feel grateful to have lived with and influenced the young people who were my students and who are now adults with their own families, with whom we maintain bonds of friendship and affection. But above all, I am grateful for the opportunity offered to me through this project, to give, although I believe I receive more, even now, from this great family.

I will always be in favour of inclusive education for deaf students integrated into regular schools, provided that they can count on provision of language therapy, hearing aids and assistance from staff who know sign language so that they can indeed participate in everything the schools offer.

8

Classes: Communication is everything

Sign Language at the Lakeside School

The school was visited by many travellers from the snowy north, especially during the tourist season at Lakeside. What really surprised almost everyone was finding that the sign language in use in Mexico was different to American Sign Language (ASL) which most thought was the universal language of the deaf. I used to point out that even in Canada there are two distinct sign languages: ASL in English-speaking Canada and Langue des Signes Quebecoise (LSQ), used in Francophone Canada. Worldwide, there are well over 100 different sign languages.

Mexican Sign Language (LMS in Spanish) is believed to have derived from Old French Sign Language which combined with pre-existing local sign languages when deaf schools were first established in Mexico in the 1860s. (The French occupied Mexico, 1862–1867.) It is mutually unintelligible with ASL. Perhaps 90% of the signs are different; however, both sign languages use the same manual alphabet. LMS is also unrelated to Spanish Sign Language, used in Spain. LMS was officially declared a "national language" of Mexico, along with Spanish and the indigenous languages, in 2005.

The history of the use of sign language at the school is a slightly complicated story. As related in chapter 1, Jackie and Roma initially tried teaching the children through oral and written Spanish. Then the young man from El Salvador introduced American signs, which staff started using with the Spanish language, and the children's communication improved rapidly.

When Susan van Gurp and I arrived in September 1982, we assumed that American signs were in general use in Mexico, as in El Salvador. An early visit to the government primary school for the deaf in Guadalajara did not alert us to our misconception since the school was still working with oral language only (and generally without the benefit of student hearing aids).

It was not until May 1984 that Susan happened to meet some deaf adults in Guadalajara and discovered they were using Mexican Sign Language, with signs almost entirely different to American Sign Language. The following month, Javier—an oral, hard of hearing young man from Guadalajara—donated two weeks of his time to introduce Mexican signs to our school. The students adapted quickly and didn't seem particularly phased by this change. As a thank-you gift, I fitted Javier with a donated hearing aid and he was thrilled to be able to hear better.

When new staff were employed, they would attend Saturday morning sign classes in Guadalajara, presented by members of the *Asociación de Silentes*, the deaf community's social club. There was no dictionary of Mexican Sign Language available in the mid-1980s, so these classes were our main means of expanding our sign vocabulary.

In 1987 we created our own small handbook of basic signs which we photocopied for families to use at home. Also in 1987, Dr. Freeman King, working with members of the *Asociación de Silentes*, completed a video teaching Mexican Sign Language step by step, for use by our parents and new staff, with copies made available to other institutions. This was probably the first such video in Mexico.

Saturday morning sign classes for local families were initiated by teacher Sara in early 1985, and I reactivated them on my return later that year. Both adults and children attended and the eight bravest members of the class agreed to present a signed carol at the 1986 Christmas concert. As the boarding program grew,

Teacher Linda and María Elena reading together

I also offered weekly sign classes, for an hour or so at noon on Fridays, when family members came to pick up their children for the weekend. Later, when our early intervention program began, teacher Citlali taught sign language to the mothers while the 2- and 3-year-olds joined some kindergarten activities.

Total Communication

During the 1970s, '80s and '90s, most schools and programs for deaf children in the developed world supported the educational philosophy known as Total Communication, which was seen as a bridge between an oral-only philosophy and a philosophy that embraced sign language. It is an approach that incorporates all means of communication: formal signs, fingerspelling, listening, lip-reading, speech and written language. The goal was to optimize language development in whatever way was most effective for the individual child.[10]

In the classroom, this took the form of "simultaneous communication", with the teacher speaking and signing at the same time. Thus our teachers used Mexican signs in Spanish language word order as they spoke.

Class composition

Because we were happy to enrol any student, from 2-year-olds up to young adults, regardless of their communication abilities or month of arrival, our class composition was often quite fluid as we tried to accommodate a wide range of ages and abilities in small, manageable classes. North of the border in schools for the deaf the maximum class size was typically six students in the primary years, maybe seven in high school, with a teaching assistant added for kindergarten groups or special needs students. Our classes, too, were usually kept in this same teacher-pupil ratio, but the students in a class might sometimes have a five-year age range, particularly when the school was smaller and operated fewer classes.

By the early 1990s we were running a variety of classes for 40–45 students. The small pre-kinder, "early intervention" group of 2- to 3-year-olds joined the junior kindergarten class for a few hours twice a week. The five children in each of our junior and senior kindergarten classes of 3–7-year-olds were helped with their development of language and general skills by former students (Francisca and Lourdes) employed as teaching assistants, as well as by their kindergarten teachers.

The primary school-age children were grouped into three classes of six or seven students, never larger, whilst the senior class of older teenagers and young adults, with varying years of schooling and different degrees of hearing loss, numbered seven or occasionally eight. From 1989 on, we always had six full classes operating.

In addition, teacher Elizabeth began providing intensive speech and language tutorials for 1½ hours each morning for four or five of our severely deaf students who were integrated into local primary schools in the afternoon sessions. These were students whose reading, writing, mathematics and comprehension of speech had developed to the point where they were able to be successful in the large classes and regular curriculum in local schools, when provided with hearing aids and given continued daily support at the Lakeside School. Teacher Elizabeth also worked with the kindergarten class to help initiate voice production and with selected older students who had the potential to develop intelligible speech.

Student attendance was always remarkably good in all the classes and the children were always happy to be back after weekends and holidays.

Teaching language to deaf children

The majority of the school-age children who studied at the Lakeside School were previously un-schooled and had only home-made signs and gestures for communication. These children generally quickly learned the signs, and later the printed words, for common objects, action verbs and some adjectives and adverbs. It is easy to teach the signs for "house, banana, run, jump, sour, cold, good " if you provide enough visual examples.

But gaining an understanding of arbitrary or abstract concepts is a very different learning task; for example, the signs and spoken words for questions and time—"Who? What? How? Why? Yesterday; next May; 12 years old"—held no meaning for most new arrivals. And, except for basic short sentences, mastering word order and grammatical structures to read and write more advanced Spanish was a daunting task for these deaf students and a huge educational challenge for their teachers. A classic study of oral teaching programs in the UK in 1979 showed that half the deaf children leaving school at age 16 had a median reading age of nine years (Grade 3), despite an early start; such is the barrier that deafness can create for language mastery.[11]

Kindergarten hearing children generally understand basic time concepts because they have heard them used in context so many times since birth. "It's Sunday tomorrow, so Grandpa will

Teacher Gaby's junior kindergarten practising speech sounds

be here for lunch." "You rode the new bike last week, so it's Lucy's turn today." Hearing children take for granted our arbitrary division of time into weeks of seven days and the ordered naming of the days.

Our deaf children, maybe 8 or 12 years old on enrolment, had never heard those casual family conversations embedded with time concepts and general information about daily life and the wider world, nor had they been able to clearly ask questions and understand the answers until they arrived at the Lakeside School. Rare is the parent who can give the extra time and effort, and has the signing skills, to fully include the deaf child in daily conversations. Our students needed to learn through structured, creative teaching lots of things which are common knowledge to hearing children.

As one of the characters in the comic strip *Peanuts* once said, "Happiness is having something to look forward to."

If a family has only a few home-made signs and thus very limited communication with their deaf child, then that child misses out on the joy of anticipation.

A typical day at the Lakeside School

A school newsletter to supporters in March 1991 described a typical day at the school:

LAKESIDE SCHOOL FOR THE DEAF ESCUELA PARA SORDOS DE JOCOTEPEC A.C.

PRIVADA   GONZALEZ ORTEGA · APARTADO 79 · JOCOTEPEC, 45800 JALISCO, MEXICO

Dear Friends:

Many of you have been generously supporting the Lakeside School for the Deaf for many years without being able to visit us, so in this newsletter we'll try to give you a picture of daily life at the school.

8.15 am. The March sky is cloudless as the first of the 42 students arrive. Juan Luis and Juan Diego kick pebbles along the cobblestone street, glad to be off the bus after a one-hour ride along the lakeshore from Chapala.

At the school gate, they and the other dozen bus riders stop to chat in sign language with ex-student, now maintenance man, José, as he parks the school station wagon. Out tumbles a crowd of 4- to 8-year-olds collected by José from homes and boarding homes on the other side of town.

Now some of the little ones race for the new infant swings while a select group of children head to the kitchen where Clara, our young cook, is preparing a fortified milk drink to supplement whatever breakfast they've eaten at home.

8:30 Teachers are checking the sets of classroom amplifiers which have been recharging overnight. The children strap them to their chests and insert their individually-made ear molds. They don't complain that the system is somewhat bulky since they realize the aid brings the teacher's voice to them strongly, regardless of where she moves with the cordless FM radio microphone.

Now their individual behind-the-ear aids are checked and stored in glass jars until the children put them back on to go home in the afternoon.

"Are your aids working?" asks teacher Elizabeth in the level 3 class. "Listen for your name. Alejandro."

"Present", calls a 6-year-old boy, clearly.

"Paty", calls the teacher. Two girls raise their hands, one incorrectly.

"Listen again, Yanet", says Elizabeth.

For some students, speech discrimination is a very difficult skill to acquire, especially if they are profoundly deaf and were without schooling or a hearing aid until late childhood, as is the case with many of our students, like 11-year-old Yanet.

Calendar work follows. In our level 1 class (6–8-year-olds), new students, like Misael, sit wide-eyed and puzzled as the "old hands" vie for the right to announce the day and place the date slip in the correct slot in the teacher-made calendar.

"Yes. Today is Thursday", models teacher Citlali, and the children repeat the signed sentence and approximate the speech. They talk about what is happening in class today.

"And what day was yesterday?" asks Citlali.

With the help of sketches of class activities drawn yesterday on the flip chart, the children are helped to form simple sentences beginning, "Yesterday we..." And then they move on to naming yesterday and confirming that tomorrow is Friday.

Teacher Citlali adds, "Tomorrow Misael's mother will come to school. *Mamá* will hug Misael. They will go home in the bus." There's a shy smile from Misael once he grasps the communication, and nods of agreement from his classmates.

"News time" is a popular daily activity in most schools for the deaf. In the junior kindergarten, everyone is examining a gash on newly-enrolled Victor's leg while he uses a mixture of signs, mime and voice to tell what happened. Teacher Gaby models some simple sentences for him. "Now, tell us again,

Calendar time: Chavalito signing "martes" (Tuesday)

Victor," and Gaby helps him with some new signs and speech approximation.

A class of 7- to 10-year-olds is signing their news and may need help organizing sentence structure before teacher Lupita writes it on the blackboard. "The brother of Esther went to the USA yesterday. Her mother cried." Eventually the class will read all the students' news items, signing and with speech approximation.

Meanwhile, in the level III class, one student has written the full date in words across the top of the blackboard and now 13-year-old Cuca, with three years at the school, is writing her news below the date. *"Ayer Angélica, Martha, Carolina yo trabajamos dulces."* (Yesterday, A, M, C [and] I worked [making] candies").

The four girls have been offered a few hours work each week by one of our parents who makes and sells candies. Teacher Nena suggests that they save some of their small earnings to purchase macramé materials for a Mother's Day gift they can make in teacher Chela's craft class. Another student writes that she is tired. She got up at 6.00am. She ironed clothes for the family. Then she came to school.

At mid-morning there is a wide range of activities going on. The kinder class has welcomed 2-year-olds Doris, Mayela, and Arturo who, with their mothers, join the group each Tuesday and Thursday. Now the children are re-enacting their recent trip in a local bus to the next village. It's an opportunity to practise voice production, and all except Arturo are enthusiastically chanting "*bú, bú, bú,*" as they bounce around the room clutching onto a big cardboard cut-out of a bus (made by teacher Gaby) and picking up "passengers" who must remember to wave down the bus, pay the driver and get their ticket.

Later, some of the senior kindergarten children practise forming letters, or copying their own name, in a visual-tactile medium, by printing with a finger in a layer of salt in a cookie tray. If they make an error, they just shake the tray, laughing, and try again. The local sand was too coarse for a sand tray.

In the next room, a class is playing a vocabulary game: matching word cards to pictures, then printing their new vocabulary words. They must memorize the spelling of whole words since they cannot hear complete words and so cannot sound-out the words, letter by letter, the way Mexican hearing children learn to read Spanish words whose sound and meaning they already know. Meanwhile, teacher Elizabeth works on spoken language with 8-year-old Carmen, who is not profoundly deaf. Her speech is easily understood but her sentence structures are like those of a 2-year-old. She has come a long way since she started school 15 months ago and received her first hearing aid. Now the question is: Can we get her ready for a regular afternoon Grade 1 class in a local school by September, as her family would like? The Lakeside School would provide speech and language assistance each morning.

One class is outside practising for the upcoming Jalisco Deaf School Olympics that our school is hosting at the end of the month. Senior student César, 20, leads the warm-up exercises whilst teacher Lupita questions young boarder Mario about his lack of tennis shoes, despite several requests to parents in the students' weekly news sheet, *Escúchame* (Listen to Me).

"Mamá no tiene dinero" (Mum doesn't have any money) signs 8-year-old Mario, famous for his infectious smile and his eyes, one blue, one brown.

Digging in his pocket, Mario produces some pesos—what remains of his weekly pocket money—and offers them all to Lupita, signing, "Gwen buy tennis shoes, please." He knows it isn't nearly enough but it's all he has and he does want those shoes so he can run in the Olympics. And so we will arrange for Mario and several other students to get bargain basement tennis shoes and white shorts, thanks to our Sponsorship program and Mario's small sacrifice.

Meanwhile, seven students aged 11–14 are engrossed in a collection of books illustrating the Life of Early Man. On a table is their 3D model of some prehistoric animal life. Tomorrow, with teacher Linda's guidance, they will write about Man the Hunter and next week visit the Regional Museum in Guadalajara. But right now it's time for one of their last music classes for the year with volunteer teacher Betty who will return to the US at the end of the winter snowbird season. As the students are reading music and playing the recorder and percussion instruments, a group of visitors on a tour of the school applauds their fine effort.

The eight students in the senior class (aged 15–20) are reviewing a science unit before their test tomorrow on the basic functioning of the human digestive system and related practical health issues. They are looking forward to next week's science classes when they'll be introduced to the school's donated microscope by teacher Nena. One student asks which day they will begin the self-defence course that Nena has promised to teach, one session a week for two months.

11:30 Snack Time. The kindergarten children have already eaten their morning snack of soya burgers and a favourite Mexican salad of cucumber, *jicama* and orange. Teaching assistant Francisca, an ex-student, insisted that each ask correctly for their food and drink and helped them recall the names of the fruit and vegetables in their salad.

Now the other students collect their snack and sit around the garden patio, eating and exchanging news. Then they head to the new multi-purpose court where Meche, the school secretary, and César supervise the basketball practice.

In the noon-time math classes, the younger teenagers are working with long multiplication and long division, but it is the interpretation of the word problems that causes the most trouble. Two young adults, previously unschooled, are making change in mock purchasing transactions, using stacks of real coins and imitation paper money, then writing down the correct answers.

Meanwhile, some 7- to 9-year-olds are in the kitchen pouring water into containers... *"Es menos que un litro. Es mas que un litro."* (It is less than... more than a litre). The concept of a litre is understood but they have to memorize the spelling and word order for this language.

They will practise reading, writing and using this structure again tomorrow and the day after, and next week too, in different contexts in math and Spanish classes—*"Juan es mas alto que Paty"* (word-for-word translation "Juan is more tall than Paty"); "Juan tiene menos dinero que Paty." (Juan has less money than Paty"). When the water boils, the class makes a litre of jello, then it's back to their Spanish language Grade 2 math textbooks, brought in from the US because the language used is easier for our students to understand than the language in the Mexican school texts.

After math, students help tidy the classrooms and put on their personal hearing aids. It's time to catch the bus, get a ride in the school vehicle or walk the now hot streets to their houses, ready to eat lunch (*comida*), the main meal of the day, served from 2:00 to 3:00pm in the afternoon.

Vocational classes

The Lakeside School needed to create future employment opportunities for adolescent students by providing vocational training and promoting employment skills.

From April 1987 to 1994 a paid, part-time dressmaking teacher instructed in pattern making, dressmaking and hand decoration of garments. Commercial paper patterns were unobtainable, so students learnt to design, measure and make their own. Some students later made a living in commercial or home-based dressmaking businesses.

Senior boys benefited from a series of classes in electricity given by a high school teacher in 1987. The practical side of the course gave us new lights and more power outlets in the school and in the lean-to carpentry workshop. By 1990 a woodworking class was once again being taught, this time by volunteer Jim Manning. Well-crafted footstools were the first project. For the senior girls, a basic hairdressing course was organized, with the offer of more advanced vocational training for anyone interested.

Also that year, students in two classes were enthralled by a series of papier-mâché mask-making classes given by nationally-exhibited mask-maker Tomás Reza, who volunteered his time at the school. The results were exceptionally good. Some masks were hung for decoration in the school, while others were sold to raise funds.

In October 1992 several popular new teaching projects began, offering afternoon classes with a focus on employment skills, taught by volunteer Canadian instructors and financed by a generous donation from the Catholic Diocese of Mackenzie in northern Canada. (chapter 12)

Under the supervision of Canadian horticulturalist Marie Pruden, the horticulture project created a 320-square-metre organic vegetable garden at the school. The land was tractor-plowed by a volunteer and rotor-tilled by students; even pint-sized Mario, star of the school video, learned to control the heavy rotor-tiller. Before Christmas, each student had seeds sprouting in recycled milk containers and these were then transplanted and carefully hand-tended in raised beds. Harvesting of 16 different vegetables began in April 1993.

All students aged 10 and up were rostered on a volunteer basis to work one afternoon a week in the garden. The children were so enthusiastic about the project that many regularly turned up three or four afternoons a week to help and learn. All looked forward to eating the harvest and learning how to store and preserve some of the vegetables. Marie also taught senior students about planting and pruning fruit trees and caring for existing citrus trees and edible cacti. Thanks to Mr. Young, also from the Mackenzie Diocese project, a new water system was installed from the well to the vegetable garden and orchard areas.

Jewelry and art classes, another project of the Canadian team, were taught by artist volunteer Wendee Hill. Six classes of enthusiastic students (ages 6 and up) learned the techniques for producing attractive, casual, modern jewelry using locally available materials. Wendee also had the students experimenting with the basics of art and design: colour, texture and form. The students created their own art folios of painting and printing techniques—like wonderfully messy potato prints—learned in class during the week.

Senior students could attend afternoon jewelry workshops, designing and making beautiful, saleable pieces. Wendee also worked directly with the teachers as they aimed to jointly produce a Spanish language teachers' manual for classroom art education.

In 1993 the Mackenzie Diocese Outreach Project also funded construction of a simple, secure carpentry workshop, where carpentry classes continued, now led by Mr. Young.

Work experience

By 1992 our extracurricular program also included Work Experience Placements. Some senior students were learning (a lot) and earning (a little) in the afternoons and on Saturday mornings:

In a plant nursery, Bertha was learning to classify plants, seed, transplant, prune and so on, thanks to Marie Pruden and Ajijic nursery owner Alejandro Treviño.

In a Mexican potter's workshop, Juan Diego helped make and paint traditional clay ornaments and vases, thanks to parents of a kindergarten student.

In an ironworkers shop, Juan Luis was learning to shape and solder wrought iron furniture, thanks to teacher Elizabeth and her husband.

In a Jocotepec carpentry workshop, one or two teenagers were learning to make furniture and wooden educational equipment, four afternoons a week, thanks to Citlali's husband.

Four older students helped with production and shipping in a high-end ceramics factory on paid, partial-afternoon shifts, thanks to Billy Moon who praised them as excellent workers. They discovered their manager had a deaf toddler, Pedro, who enrolled in our infant stimulation program with his mother in September 1993.

In the school garden, Eduardo was learning to be a skilled gardener and to supervise younger student "workers", thanks to Marie Pruden and a committee member who provided a small weekly "wage". Two years later, after finishing his schooling, Eduardo quickly found work at a large vegetable exporting agro-business near his home town. His manager appreciated the skills and knowledge he arrived with and soon rated him as one of his best employees.

Two senior boys ran their own key-cutting business in the afternoons for a time, using a donated machine and rent-free space, in a store on the main street of Jocotepec owned by the father of fellow deaf student, León. Their math teacher made sure they learned how to keep basic small-business accounts.

Life after school

In the 1980s I saw deaf youths and adults trying to eke out a living selling key chains and other trinkets on the streets of Guadalajara, handing out cards explaining "I am deaf." As far as we (former Lakeside School staff) are aware, our ex-students have never had to resort to a precarious life on the street.

Today, several former students own cars and run their own small businesses in Jocotepec (auto painting, windshield coating and replacement, commercial cleaning) or Los Angeles (house painting); some work as independent gardeners in Lakeside homes; some own or help manage their family's small but profitable farms; others work in specialized construction or as bricklayers.

The hospitality industry in California, and locally at Lakeside, provides stable employment for some as cooks or hotel staff. One of the school's first female students has brought up two sons as a single mother whilst working continuously for over 30 years at the hotel La Nueva Posada in Ajijic. Some girls have worked for a time as dressmakers in commercial and home-based businesses, or as staff at large retail outlets, while many have married and are bringing up successful, well-educated children; a few are even helping with grandchildren now.

9

Individual stories: New students, 1989–1994

Miriam

Miriam had just turned 3 when she started in our kinder in October 1989. However, she and her mother had been receiving home instruction from our staff for a year prior to this. We had fitted Miriam with a donated hearing aid and enrolled her mother in the Spanish-language version of the renowned John Tracy Clinic (Los Angeles) correspondence course for families of pre-school deaf children. Miriam's mother had followed suggestions for language development and play at home, encouraging her little one to vocalize, to watch faces and lips and to identify the sounds she was able to hear. But, with four other children at home, she couldn't devote the immense amount of time required for an oral program to succeed.

In the summer of 1989, Miriam's aunt, who lived in Los Angeles, paid the bus fare for mother and child to visit the John Tracy Clinic. There, the audiologist confirmed the Guadalajara test that showed Miriam to be profoundly deaf, and recommended she continue using the hearing aid we had adapted for her. The family was told there was no medical intervention that could help Miriam. This satisfied her mother who had, like most mothers of deaf children, hoped that there might be some "cure".

So Miriam started attending our kinder class from 9.00am to 1.00pm daily. Her motor skills and fine motor co-ordination were good for her age. She learned quickly and soon started to use her first signs. All the staff insisted that she vocalize an approximation of the words when learning new vocabulary, and when she wanted to tell us something, though she could not hear the full range of speech sounds, even with her hearing aid.

Miriam's father hadn't really reached the stage of accepting that his daughter was profoundly deaf by the time she began kinder class and, at first, resisted the idea of using sign language. He worked from home making small quantities of sweets that he sold to local stores. It was not a very profitable business and there were five children to care for, Miriam being the youngest. The family lived very simply and could never have afforded a hearing aid for Miriam.

Because she was a bright child and started her specialized education at an appropriate age, Miriam had every possibility of becoming a literate, knowledgeable young woman.

When Miriam married, her hearing husband asked some of her former teachers for help to learn sign language, concerned to help his wife in any way he could. They have a young deaf daughter to care for.

Luis, a natural leader

Luis had just turned 4 when he arrived in January 1990. He and his single mother, Guillermina, walked for two hours from grandfather's little farm in the mountains, on the other side of Lake Chapala, to the nearest town, then took two buses to reach Jocotepec. They carried their entire belongings for their new life in a single canvas bag. Their arrival was a complete surprise to the staff.

I spent the afternoon seeking help in finding them somewhere to live, but without success. They slept in the school for two nights before staff found humble one-room accommodation for them and an American friend, Russell Bayly, offered to employ Guillermina as a maid.

Luis was not used to electric light and just lived for a ride in a car, a novelty for him. He had a lot to learn as he did little communicating; we even had to teach him to wave goodbye. But he was a bright little boy and started to use his first signs—"cookie", "water", "car"—after a few weeks in school. His mother was literate and had once worked in an office in Guadalajara. Luis was fortunate that she sought help early and was prepared to leave the extended family and their *rancho* for the sake of her son's future.

Luis completed Grade 6 at the school in his mid-teens, before working at whatever jobs were available and carefully saving his money. His first big purchase was a fully paid-for new red scooter, a popular form of transport around town. Now, in 2019, he owns a car and (with signing translation help from one of his former teachers) has obtained his driver's license. He runs his own successful commercial cleaning business with clients in Guadalajara and Lakeside, and also works evenings at weekends for a Jocotepec taco restaurant where the regulars enjoy his friendly, humorous service.

With advice and some help from Russell, Guillermina's long-term employer, Luis planned and gradually built a house for his mother and is now adding a second story, working on the construction at weekends with another former student, Victor, who is now a bricklayer.

Today, Luis is recognized as a natural leader and organizer of the deaf community in the area, a very social, hardworking and helpful young man who successfully communicates with everybody, by one means or another.

Family F: Martha, Josefina, Carmen and Gilberto

These four siblings came from Las Pintas, a small village near Guadalajara airport. (see their mother's story in chapter 3)

When we met Martha, 13, in January 1991 she had already "completed" Grade 6 in her village school and at first was not enthusiastic about starting school again. However, after a couple of weeks, it was clear that she enjoyed the "one big family" setting at the Lakeside School.

Martha, with a profound hearing loss, was the deafest of the three sisters and the only one to have worn a hearing aid. She could say or repeat some individual words, but did not speak in sentences. Martha had not learned to read or write anything other than her name, although she could copy neatly. In her first weeks at our school, she had to learn very basic vocabulary, like the names of colours and the order of the days of the week, in sign language, print and speech.

Martha was a willing worker and made steady, though not rapid, progress. Our aim was always to give her basic life skills to enable her to live more independently than would have been the case if she had remained at home doing housework during her adolescent years. Over the next three or four years, she attained very basic literacy—enough to read and write a simple note—improved her spoken communication; mastered enough practical math to handle money in daily life; and learned to tell the time and to understand the calendar, a simple map, basic health, sex education and so on.

Josefina was 10 and unable to read when she arrived at the school in 1991. Like her younger sister, she was a smart student, who worked hard, learned quickly and had a strong personality. Because of her age, she was not integrated into Grade 1, like her younger siblings, but continued as a full-time student in Linda's class in 1993-94.

Carmen started at the Lakeside School two weeks before her 7th birthday, which was celebrated by the whole school. She had never been to kindergarten and, because of her severe hearing loss, some of her "kinder skills" were poorly developed. She could say only a couple of words like "mamá, papá," but had a pleasant speaking voice. As she learned to pronounce new words, now with a hearing aid, she could be easily understood, which is not always the case with severely deaf children.

A bright young girl, Carmen learned quickly in her first six months at school, mastering a basic sign vocabulary that allowed her to communicate better with her sisters and other students, using formal sign language to ask and answer questions. Returning after the summer holidays in 1991 to a class of six students all about her age, she was working on beginning reading and writing, Grade 1 math, and courses in social studies and nature study centred on the local area.

By September 1992, Carmen was able to be integrated, with special help, into Grade 1 in a local primary school. In the mornings, from 8.30 to 10.00am, she attended the Lakeside School for intensive speech and language work with teacher Elizabeth and two other students. From 2.00 to 6.30pm she joined the afternoon primary school. Her results that first year were very good; she followed the same schedule for Grade 2, before continuing her education back in her local school.

Gilberto joined his three sisters as a boarder in Jocotepec in September 1993, aged 7. His mother had hoped he might cope in his local primary school, but was told he would have to repeat Grade 1 because he hadn't learned to "read" any Spanish using the phonetic teaching system. So she enrolled him at the Lakeside School, in our special speech and language tutorial group, working with teacher Elizabeth each morning. In the afternoon, he attended Grade 1 in a regular Jocotepec school, just as his sister, Carmen, had done the previous year. Gilberto was moderately to severely deaf. With a hearing aid and the individualized attention each morning, his speech became quite clear, although it was a long time before he was speaking in full sentences. His schedule of integration with support worked sufficiently well that he was able to transfer back to his home school in 1995.

Armando

New arrivals in September 1991 included a brother and sister, Armando, 13, and Laura, 15 (not their real names). Profoundly deaf, from an impoverished rural family, they had suffered all their lives

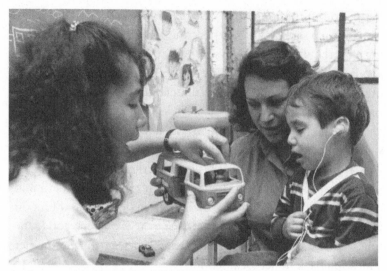

Early intervention. While his mother watches, Gaby encourages 2-year-old Arturo C. to vocalize

under a physically abusive father. Indeed, their mother reportedly believed that their deafness had been caused by their father giving them blows to the head.

Finally, in the summer of 1991, the mother fled the situation, placing her four malnourished children in the care of *Niños y Jovenes* children's home. Their mother left no forwarding address and never returned. The youngsters were dropped off at the Lakeside School one Monday morning. They had no documentation because the secretary at the home had not arrived with the keys to the file cabinet. Since they could not speak or write, they were unable to tell us even their names.

Armando started using Mexican signs immediately and made rapid progress in communication. Once fitted with amplification, he liked to try approximating spoken words. He was eager to learn, always completed his homework, and even asked for more. Given the upheaval he had recently been through, he settled into school life remarkably well. Workers at the children's home reported that he and his siblings had appeared startled and apprehensive on arrival by such things as electricity. The next two years at the school certainly broadened his world and gave him basic life skills. In summer of 1993, after their mother died, the head of the home—Padre Macías—sent the two deaf teenagers to Mexico City, their birth place, but Armando and his sister later returned on their own, not to the children's home but to live with friends near Jocotepec. Armando began working in the local berry-exporting business and is now a permanent employee there. He is reportedly doing well, lives in a nearby village with his partner, a hearing woman, and has a good relationship with his deaf sister who lives and works in Jocotepec. They meet regularly in the Jocotepec plaza to exchange news.

Arturo, our first student to graduate from university

Two-year-old Arturo entered the Early Intervention Program at the Lakeside School in January 1992. Arturo, Doris, also aged 2 and Mayela, just turned 3, joined the kinder class for a few hours every Tuesday and Thursday.

In August 1992 Arturo's mother, along with parents of two other young deaf children, accompanied teachers Lupita and Aby to a five-day parent education seminar presented by the John Tracy Clinic of Los Angeles. The course was held in the neighbouring state of San Luis Potosí.

Arturo's twin brother, Álvaro, a hearing child, accompanied Arturo when he started full time kinder classes at the Lakeside School in September 1992. Together they learned sign language which gave Arturo access to the vocabulary and concepts of kindergarten children, and together they mastered the other normal kindergarten skills. Arturo was profoundly deaf, bright and artistically talented.

With the support of his twin, he later completed primary school and then graduated from the Junior High School in Jocotepec. Arturo opened the door for special support for deaf students at

Junior High school and at CETAC (the senior high technical school). Teacher Manuel López, working from the Special Education Centre/Lakeside School, was able to assist Arturo and other deaf students, like Susana Ureña, with their studies at CETAC, in consultation with staff.

Arturo later gained admission to the "Artes Plásticas" (Fine Arts) program at the University of Guadalajara, where he studied part-time and specialized in drawing and painting. His brother Álvaro was able to offer support at first. For his final two years of study, Arturo relied on friends for assistance in the language-based academic areas.

In 2018, in their village of Potrerillos, his family celebrated his graduation as a Bachelor of Fine Arts. Former Lakeside School teachers Manuel López, Gaby Escamilla and Citlali Bravo were invited guests and gave signed translation of the special mass and celebratory speeches for the Lakeside School's first university graduate.

Arturo immediately gained employment at the Jocotepec Cultural Centre and is currently brightening the town with lively murals and other artistic decorations.

Family M: Bertha, Cuca, Ana Rosa and José de Jesús

Sr. M. and his wife had nine children, four of whom were profoundly deaf. They arrived at the school at the end of June 1992, having been referred by DIF Jalisco (State Family Services), seeking to enrol the deaf children—Bertha aged 15, Cuca 11, Ana Rosa 9 and José de Jesús 5—for the start of term in September. The teachers agreed to squeeze the four children into our already full classes but our problem then was to find accommodation without splitting them up.

The father was a poor farmer and the family lived at close to subsistence level outside a tiny village in the Jalisco mountains. To get to school, they had to leave at 5.00am and walk several kilometres before taking the first of three buses to arrive at Jocotepec shortly after 9.00am. By the time the parent returned home, most of the working day had passed and the cost of transportation had reached almost US$30, equivalent to six days pay at the minimum wage in Mexico at the time. Obviously, in terms of both time and money, the family could not afford to bring the children each Monday and return for them each Friday.

We were able to solve the accommodation problem to the parent's satisfaction by initially placing the three girls in the *Niños y Jovenes* (Children and Youth) children's home in San Juan Cosalá, and having the little boy board with the family of one of his kinder classmates, Mayela, since he was too young for the children's home. The children returned home every third or fourth weekend. Even this arrangement caused major economic difficulties for the family, but the parents missed their children and wanted to see them at least once a month.

Having students reside in *Niños y Jovenes* was not ideal as there was little adult supervision for their 180 children. However, one of the senior girls, Lety, attended sign classes at our school in order to be able to communicate more effectively with the deaf children she supervised.

The three sisters had each attended a rural primary school for a couple of grades and could copy words but didn't know what they meant. They used some home-made signs for limited communication. In math, Bertha could add single digits, but her sisters still had to learn to relate written numbers and objects up to 10. Jesús had never been to kinder but, except for language, had fairly well developed skills for his age.

All four children were eager to return to school after their first weekend at home in late September. They had found, in the classrooms and playground, a world where communication was becoming possible for the first time in their lives. With hearing aids, speech and signs, they started learning basic language skills: how to name things instead of just pointing; how to ask questions and grasp the answers; how to understand time and the calendar;

how to tell personal news and express ideas; and how to name emotions, eventually in signed sentences and written words.

In 1993 the four children were able to move to a modern, two-story house in Jocotepec, where they boarded for several years with Canadian volunteer teachers Wendee and Marie while they continued their schooling. At age 18, Bertha returned to the family farm and now works in cottage industries to help support her own family. Cuca is now married with her own two children, while Jesús, known as a gentle-natured young man, works on the high scaffolding on construction sites.

Ana Rosa earned her Grade 6 certificate at the school in Jocotepec, then completed Junior High School at the school for the deaf in Zapopan in suburban Guadalajara. Weekdays, she was a boarder in the city; she returned every weekend to stay with Wendee and Marie. Ana Rosa married a fellow student from the Zapopan school. She kept in close contact with Wendee whom she regarded as her second mother. Ana Rosa, her husband and their two bright, teenage (hearing) children were sponsored by Wendee and her husband to experience an eye-opening winter vacation in 2014 with them at their home in Alberta, Canada. Ana Rosa can communicate in Mexican and American sign languages, and can read and write both Spanish and basic English. The Lakeside School truly opened new worlds for her.

10

A wider world: Field trips and special visits

Experiencing first-hand the world outside the classroom and the family home was vitally important for the education of our students. Experience-based language, science, history and geography lessons flowed from excursions and extracurricular activities, as students learned the signed, spoken and written words to describe what they saw, the facts and concepts they learned, and the emotions they felt.

Our students would never have been able to participate in these life-expanding activities had it not been for a core of dedicated volunteers, a school committee raising funds to cover costs, provision of transportation by volunteer drivers and, above all, the extraordinary amount of unpaid time and effort provided by the teachers in expertly planning and supervising all the out-of-class learning.

As a result, the Lakeside School's students were, in fact, a lucky group in terms of their participation in enriching extracurricular experiences compared with most of their local hearing peers and most deaf students in the rest of the state.

What follows are just some of the extracurricular activities, excursions and experiences the school was able to organize. Many were one-off events; some were activities on offer for years.

Swimming classes began in 1983 and continued for many years, thanks to the generosity of Phyllis and Georg Rauch. Students were always enthusiastic about their Friday morning swimming lessons

A junior kindergarten excursion: (L-R) Luis Fernando, Miriam, Lupita, Alejandro, Oswaldo

every second week in the Rauchs' large outdoor, solar-heated pool within walking distance of the school. Staff taught even the most water-wary students to swim and added swimming races as more gained mastery. Given the many swimming locations in the area—the lake shore and various public thermal pools—these classes imparted a lifelong recreational skill.

Horseback riding in Chapala was a big success in early 1984. Volunteers running a therapeutic riding centre provided a series of sessions which allowed our students to feel more comfortable on and around horses.

A trip to the circus in Ajijic was a highlight of the following year, thanks to Morley Eager of La Nueva Posada providing tickets and transport for the evening event. The students were enchanted by the acts in the big tent and, like Morley, were huge fans of the circus elephant.

Our senior students enjoyed a really memorable evening trip to Guadalajara's Degollado Theatre in May 1986 to see the visiting American Theatre of the Deaf perform mime and signed dramas.

The annual Octoberfest (*Fiestas de Octubre*) in Guadalajara celebrates the traditional arts, crafts, music, games and foods of Jalisco. Thanks to volunteer drivers, all students were able to spend a fun-filled day at this cultural exhibition in 1986. They learned about some of the traditional crafts prior to the trip, and tried making some themselves on their return.

A visit to the Guadalajara International Airport was organized in November 1986 to send-off Dr. Freeman King on his journey to Honduras. Afterwards, students had a tour of the airport, including the fire department, watched planes landing and taking off, and inspected the cabin and cockpit of an airliner. Again, this eye-opening trip for the children was made possible by early-rising volunteer drivers who collected students from their homes.

In 1989 four classes were enthralled by the monkeys, elephants and other wild life on excursions to the new Guadalajara Zoo. Committee members who kindly provided transport were impressed with the large, well-designed zoo (opened the previous year) and with the conduct of our students. The trips generated lots of language learning as the younger students made model zoos and the seniors were helped to write about their experience. And the children's favourite animal? Well, the giraffes won by a neck.

Numerous excursions were organized every year by individual classes studying particular topics. In 1990, for example, two classes aged 7 to 14, studying cities versus villages, visited central Guadalajara. Only one or two of these students had been there before, as was the case with our first trip to the state capital in 1983. Excitement ran high all day. None had ridden an escalator or been in an elevator or a hotel room before, nor seen the huge, much visited Libertad market. The senior class made two trips to Guadalajara in 1991: one to the Science Museum and Planetarium, as part of their astronomy unit, and one to view the Regional Museum when they studied prehistoric man. The highlight of the senior kindergarten's unit on mountain areas was a visit to the pine forests of

Mazamitla, 75 kilometres away. Of course, there were always many local excursions on foot to view the aquatic life of the lakeshore, building sites, medical clinics and such like which provided new material and insights for language work back in the classroom.

The committee's June 1987 newsletter reported several additional examples of special social events: "Our students thoroughly enjoyed their visits to see the fantastic tropical birds at Stan Goldburg's house in Ajijic, the clown performing at the Gould's house in Chapala and the magician at a local kindergarten."

Children's Day (*Día del Niño*) is celebrated on April 30th in every Mexican school. In 1991, thanks to free admission that day to Agua Caliente, and volunteer drivers, our students enjoyed a fun-filled day at the children's aquatic park. The following day, a party at school featured the exchange of gifts made by the students. Some classes made durable educational toys for use by a younger group and these gifts remained at school for future years.

Such social activities, together with the celebration of each child's birthday with cake and a small gift, reinforced the "one big family" atmosphere at the school. Since half our students were weekday or permanent boarders, school-based friendships and social events were particularly important. Staff special occasions were also celebrated. The six baby showers for staff, over a 12-year period, were especially joyful, with simple gifts created in class. Miraculously, our teachers' maternity leaves never overlapped.

When Tony Burton and I married during an Easter vacation, most students were unable to attend the ceremony. Returning to school, the girls said they wanted to see my wedding dress, so I went home, changed, and returned with Tony. Then I discovered that the teachers had pre-organized a mock Mexican wedding ceremony, to be held outdoors under the banana tree. A senior student, dressed as the priest, had a Spanish grammar book as his Bible. As the ceremony proceeded, the teachers explained in sign language what each custom signified. Thirteen coins (for Jesus and the 12 disciples) called *las arras*, are presented by the groom to his bride, representing his commitment to support her and their future family. The *lazo* is a long string of flowers that was placed around both our shoulders in a figure-8 to symbolize our linked future. Before cutting the cake, we held a goblet together and sipped from the same glass. Later, I threw my flower bouquet to the laughing girls and we were showered with rice for good fortune. Next time the students attended a wedding, they would better understand what they are witnessing.

As a staff, we voted not to participate in local celebrations for Mexican patriotic days; local schools spent countless hours practising marching in preparation for the parade in school uniform (which we did not have). On the only occasion we attended a Flag Day ceremony in the Jocotepec plaza, our senior students told us afterwards they had become very bored standing around for ages while dignitaries made long speeches about the history of various historic Mexican flags. That was the day the newer students first really understood the meaning of the sign for "bored".

Within the school, we always celebrated the more family-based special days. For Three Kings' Day, January 6th, when children traditionally receive gifts from the family—or rather, from the Three Kings—we always bought and shared a traditional *Rosca de Reyes*, a large wreath-shaped sweet bread, adorned with dried and candied fruit, in which is buried a tiny baby Jesus figure. Whoever gets the slice with the doll is supposed to host a party for all present, on *Día de la Candelaria* (Candlemas Day) in February. For All Saints Day/Day of the Dead, staff and students would construct a traditional altar honouring someone who had died. Those with gardens brought fresh flowers to make decorative wreaths.

Jalisco Deaf School Olympics, 1988–1993

Students from the Lakeside School competed in the 3rd annual Athletics Championships for Deaf Schools in March 1988 in Guadalajara. This was our first time competing, participation made possible by several Lakeside residents who, together with the school's teachers, volunteered time and vehicles for the two-day event. Twenty-eight Lakeside students attended amd met students from the three Guadalajara government schools for the deaf for the first time. Thirteen of our students competed (many others were too old to enter) and they carried off more than their fair share of awards. There was sufficient enthusiasm generated amongst students and staff to warrant some serious training before the next year's event.

For the readers of the *Mexico City News,* Lakeside journalist Kate Karns described the elaborately-staged opening for the event:

> The Jocotepec school once again did itself proud in March 1989 in Guadalajara. The event began with an impressive ceremony complete with a uniformed drill team proudly carrying in the Mexican flag, followed by a young girl holding aloft the Olympic torch to light the urn and start the games. To add to the excitement, doves were released to fly over the stadium and the friendly inter-school competition began.[12]

The Lakeside School students really excelled at the three-day Olympics in 1990. Over 250 competitors were registered, including 24 of our students. All the practice in the hot March–April sun paid off; we won a total of 33 medals. Our tiny teenage student Linda's gold in the 400 meter walk was one of the highlights of the track events. Our student news sheet, *Escúchame,* thanked volunteer Jim Kaye of Ajijic for helping daily with training.

In March 1991, the largest-ever Deaf School Olympics was hosted by our school in Jocotepec. The event was the sixth annual track and field meet of schools and classes for the deaf throughout the state. More than 320 students took part in a multitude of events spread over the two days.[13]

The sports were held in the Municipal Park of Jocotepec which was loaned and prepared for the occasion by the local municipality, which also lent the use of the large Municipal Auditorium for the impressive opening ceremony which featured a march past by athletes and brief speeches of welcome by the mayor, Dr. Miguel Ibarra, by teacher Citlali Bravo on behalf of the Lakeside School, and by a parent from the school who stressed the importance of "normal" social events such as these sports to children with hearing loss.

Spectators at this event said the meet had been well organized and held in an exceptionally friendly atmosphere in which students, teachers, parents and well-wishers—including many non-Mexican supporters of the Lakeside School—had all played a part. Dale and Colette Long, the official representatives of the Lakeside School Management committee, were thanked for their efficient and tireless liaison efforts that helped the event to run so smoothly. To ensure unbiased judging, staff from the school had organized a contingent of Jocotepec teachers from regular primary and secondary schools to oversee each event.

Because of the distance travelled by some schools to attend the sports, their students and staff were offered accommodation and food in Jocotepec overnight. The local Posada del Pescador welcomed a party of more than 40 students at a greatly reduced rate. Local mothers prepared supper and breakfast for the students staying overnight. The Lakeside School committee allocated the proceeds from recent Gourmet Dinners to cover the costs.

While the biggest contingents of participants were from the large schools for the deaf in Guadalajara, students also came from classes as far away as Yahualica, Arandas, La Barca, Atotonilco, Tepatitlán and even Lagos de Moreno.

The good clean country air, a vigorous training program organized by the school staff and volunteers, and the support given by the local community—both Mexican and non-Mexican—proved too much for the other schools. The 34 Lakeside competitors won a total of 42 individual medals. Even the Zapopan school, which had twice the number of competitors, failed to win as

Much used, much loved ball court

many individual medals, despite the fact that all competitors were restricted to two individual events.

The following year, in Tonalá, near Guadalajara, our 32 competitors again did exceptionally well against nearly 300 other competitors, and again won 42 medals. One of our 15-year-olds, Hector, who suffers from cerebral palsy, really tugged at everyone's heart with his showing of Olympic spirit. He entered the 400 meters walk and beat out another 15-year-old to take the bronze medal. Then he agreed to "run" a leg of the 4 X 100 meters relay so that the Lakeside School could enter a team in his age category, though Hector could hardly be said to be able to run. All four boys gave it everything they had; Hector and team took home another bronze medal.

The 1993 Olympics were held in Atotonilco, nearly three hour's drive north. We couldn't manage to attend the second day of the competitions, but even so, 80% of our students took home one or two medals.

Inauguration of Basketball Court, 1991

An Olympic basketball player was in attendance for the opening of the new basketball court on February 15, 1991. The ceremony took place on the just completed court at the school with local dignitaries, committee and parents in attendance. A plaque was unveiled, dedicating the court to Margaret Green, a volunteer assistant, who initiated the drive for funds by raising a substantial initial donation in 1990. Then Margaret threw the first ball onto the court and Howard Kelsey, who played on the 1984 Canadian Olympic team, dunked the ball before hoisting small children high above his head to take a shot.

Next, the students presented thank-you mementos to representatives of the major institutional donors, and to Jocotepec architect Lorenzo Varela who designed and supervised construction without charge. A luncheon was served featuring Jocotepec's famed barbecued goat stew (*birria*)... and the birthdays of all students born in February were celebrated with cake, ice cream and hugs.[14]

Sports are particularly important in deaf culture. Amongst deaf youths and adults around the world, there is a strong tradition of participation in team sports, perhaps because it is difficult for them to enjoy many other leisure activities like musical events, cinemas (unless sub-titled for the well-educated), TV shows and even family gatherings where everyone talks all afternoon. The new multi-purpose court (basketball, volleyball, badminton and PE games) not only stimulated fun and fitness at school, but helped us prepare students for a fuller life later.

Excursion to Villa Polynesia, 1988

Our excursion to the Pacific Ocean in April 1988 was an amazing experience for all the students. Excited shouts of "*El Mar! El Mar!*" (The sea! The sea!) filled the bus as 26 students caught their first view of the ocean. Only two of the students, who ranged in age from 3 to 24, had ever seen the ocean before and, for all of them, this was their first experience of a group excursion away from home and their families. They couldn't take their eyes off the sea once they had spotted it. For the adults accompanying the group, one of the moments that made all the planning worthwhile was seeing the youngsters marvel at a sight so many take for granted.

The three-day trip to the beach at Chamela (between Puerto Vallarta and Barra de Navidad) was made possible by the generosity of Guadalajara resident Jesús Esperanza, manager of Villa Polynesia Resort and Camping Ground. Esperanza, impressed by the work of the Lakeside School, offered free use of his extensive and well-kept facilities for as many students as would be allowed by their parents to make the trip.

Immediately on arriving at palm-fringed Chamela beach, and before unpacking the bus, the children, unable to contain their curiosity and excitement, ran across the beach, some of them wading straight into the shallow waves fully dressed, others gingerly touching the water lapping the shore, apparently to make sure it was real. Later, they were assigned to quarters in the 18 *casitas* set aside for the group's use. They then explored the two large, multi-purpose thatched *palapas* which housed the bathrooms, dining areas, cooking facilities and games rooms.

The children played in the light surf, took a long morning walk to a nearby cluster of rocks, engaged in sand castle-building, in barbequing a huge, fresh ocean fish, in late-afternoon swimming in the private pool, in roasting marshmallows at a campfire under the stars, and playing games. So involved were they in their new surroundings that none of them were a bit homesick and even the 3- and 4-year-olds didn't ask for *mamá*. All they wanted was more time on the beach.

In a mark of the trust which parents of the students have in the school, only one young girl, a new enrolee, was not given permission to go. Another family was initially unwilling to allow their teenage daughters to participate unchaperoned. That problem was resolved when their mother agreed to accompany us as a volunteer to help our staff prepare meals. Another young boy almost didn't go because he had just recovered from an illness and needed to have the final doses of his antibiotic injected (a common medical practice then). Teacher Citlali, who was qualified to give injections, offered to complete the treatment at the beach and his mother agreed.

Given that our teachers were all female, it was vital that three male volunteers—Jim Kaye, Tony Burton and Citlali's husband, Chava Vargas—accompanied the group. Apart from leadership and supervision duties, they kept a constant eye on Pedro X., our deaf and autistic youngster who was prone to wandering.

The students' experiences at Chamela provided a wealth of possibilities for additional follow-up work. An exhibition of their writing and art was later displayed at the school for visitors.

This was indeed an extraordinary event for those students. From then on they could relate, from personal experience, to images of the ocean in magazines and textbooks, in films and TV shows. Before the trip, one teenage student refused to believe that sea water was salty, having only experienced the waters of Lake Chapala. He had insisted his teacher was joking.

Deaf camp at Mazatlán, 1991

A week at camp in February 1991 created memories for a lifetime for seven students aged 12–15. They joined 60 other deaf students from Guadalajara government schools for five days at a camp, organized by the state welfare agency DIF, near Mazatlán on the Pacific coast. Our students were all enthusiastic about their first experience of socializing and living with other deaf adolescents from the big city.

American deaf students visit, 1989

In mid-June 1989, nine senior students from the Indiana School for the Deaf and their teacher, Judy Reynolds, flew in to spend two weeks with our students to learn about Mexico, Mexican sign language and practise Spanish. These deaf 17-year-olds—the academic cream of their school—were studying Spanish as a second language.

The trip was arranged and coordinated by Tony Burton, director of Odisea México AC which specialized in educational excursions. The Indiana group was largely sponsored by David Letterman, late night TV host and active supporter of the Indiana School.

The language and local cultural program was organized by Lakeside teacher Lupita and her senior students. The visitors spent five mornings in the school learning Mexican sign language and exchanging information about differences in family size, women's roles, educational opportunities and the like, with the teachers providing simultaneous signed translation in both ASL and Mexican Sign Language. To learn about village life in Mexico, the American students visited the richest mansions and the poorest dirt-floor cottages, watched men weaving and women making tortillas, and joined in the traditional Sunday night courtship parade (*paseo*) around the plaza. They also toured a state school for the deaf in Guadalajara, which they found "depressing, given the lack of hearing aids and visual material."

As well, the group made a four-day trip to the fascinating neighbouring state of Michoacán, visiting the colonial city of Pátzcuaro and Paricutín volcano. This was followed by a three-day trip to the Pacific coast at Barra de Navidad, as many of the American students had never seen the sea before. Thanks to Odisea México, our senior class of seven adolescents and two of their teachers were able to participate in these two excursions without charge.

The whole visit was an eye-opener, not only for the American students, but for our students too. The Lakeside students met, for the first time, deaf teenagers able to read and write at grade level (thanks to specialized schooling from age 2), able to sign with amazing speed and, in a few cases, able to communicate well orally. The students in our senior class that year had all begun their specialized education as teenagers and there was, consequently, a large gap between the language and conceptual levels of the two groups.

By the end of this very successful visit, plans were hatched for a possible exchange visit for some of our teachers. With free board and lodging on offer, our staff could learn a lot about specialized teaching methodology by spending a few weeks in the successful and well-equipped Indiana school with its 680 students, 130 teachers, boundless teaching materials, Olympic pool and video studio.

Visit of Mexican trainee teachers, 1990

In March 1990, having heard we were using some of the latest methods and equipment, 35 teachers-in-training studying education of the deaf in a neighbouring state, Aguascalientes, rented a bus for the day to travel the 300 kilometres to Jocotepec. They were excited by what they saw and requested copies of the many materials that we had developed over the years and which were unique to our school: specialized curriculum for the deaf adapted from a US model, language teaching handbooks which we had translated from English, our own Mexican sign language manual, our video teaching sign language, etc, etc. We were always happy to supply copies at cost to others working with deaf children in Mexico with the aim of improving the quality of education for the deaf. Our staff and students were amazed at how famous they had become!

Celebrity guests

Funding for two of the three large new classrooms officially opened in 1990 was provided by the Canadian Embassy in Mexico City. The inauguration of the new building on February 13 by Canadian Ambassador David Winfield was reported on national radio and TV and in many Jalisco newspapers. Also present were the state governor's wife—Profesora Idolina Gaona de Cosio (head of DIF Jalisco)—and several other state and local political figures.

Everyone was very impressed with the school after seeing the classes at work and then watching students participate in the official ceremonies as they performed, in sign language, the National Anthem and the Spanish version of "We Are the World." The day's good publicity appeared to benefit the school later when we sought assistance in goods and services from government institutions.

Christmas Celebrations: Santa and Christmas Concerts

The arrival of Santa with a sack full of small gifts (thanks to the school committee) was a much anticipated part of the annual Christmas party at the school. The children learned that Santa was a children's Christmas tradition from the US where many of them had relatives working. This was our only non-Mexican celebration each year, Santa having not invaded rural Mexico at that time. Consequently, a Santa suit could not be found and had to be made by a volunteer Eleonore Gould, to be worn by husband Don as the merry, gift-giving Santa.

From their inception in 1984, the annual Christmas Concerts were a highlight of the school year for students and their families, and a way of saying "Thank you" to the hardworking Lakeside friends of the school. The teachers' creativity in preparing the program each year and their willingness to invest so much after-school time—rehearsing, making props, taping music, organizing costumes (with help from some mothers and volunteer, Eleonore Gould) and constructing sets—were truly amazing.

The 1986 concert was a fantastic success—the talk of Ajijic. The two little 4-year-olds, Bety and Paty, dancing together was definitely an emotional highlight. To save money, kinder teacher Rita had made the girls' frilly dresses from J-Cloths. For the finale, there were 20 students on stage signing "Silent Night" (*Noche de Paz*), and each had at least one member of their family in attendance. There must have been some "magic" present, judging by everyone's reactions. It didn't matter that many guests had to stand, a local

Bety and Mario perform at a Christmas Concert

restaurant having failed to deliver rental chairs to the school. The following day at a large garden party in Ajijic, I was inundated by guests who, whether old-times or first-timers, had left the concert on some type of "high."

The concerts were always held on the last school day before the holidays so that family members coming to Jocotepec from afar to take children home could attend the concert on the same day. So many parents were proud and teary-eyed after watching a son or daughter perform folkloric dances in colourful costumes, play music in a recorder and percussion band, sign traditional carols, and act in a mimed comedy skit or a Mexican nativity play. From 1989 on, the concerts were staged in the lovely new Jocotepec theatre with plush tiered seating for 180 and standing room for others. Teachers Lupita and Abi kindly lent us many beautiful, expensive, multi-layered folkloric dresses for our performances in that theatre. Some years, in the week prior to the concert, students presented a short program of dances and carols for the entertainment of the old folk of Jocotepec (*Los Ancianos*) at their annual free Christmas luncheon.

Reviews of the concerts in the local press always described the concerts enthusiastically. The concert for 1990, for example, was praised as being,

> A delightfully varied program with song, dance, music, carols and even a short humorous play.... The grand finale had on stage all staff and students to perform "Silent Night." A poignant moment came when Federico Neri, 11, delivered a verbal Christmas message, "signed" by 10-year-old María Esther Morales.
>
> The audience enjoyed the concert immensely, and so did the performers! This annual event should be a 'must' on everyone's calendar. It is very warm, very moving and very joyous. If you have never seen it, then you are missing something very special.[15]

11

Hearing matters: Audiology and hearing aids

Susan van Gurp and I had, of course, completed several audiology courses at UBC prior to our move to Jocotepec. These were theoretical studies not hands-on courses, as testing children's hearing and fitting hearing aids was the role in Canada of pediatric audiologists, not teachers of the deaf. However, we realized even before leaving Vancouver that we would need to turn theory into practice in Mexico since we were carrying a class set of donated wireless FM amplifiers, teacher microphones and a large container of white powder with which to make students' ear molds for the FM system. Thankfully, Mexican customs did not inspect Susan's luggage.

Audiological services in Guadalajara in the 1980s

Unfortunately, Guadalajara in the 1980s did not provide deaf children with anywhere near the level of audiological services on offer in Vancouver. And the problem was not just in Guadalajara.

Mexican-born Regina Salomon, originally a teacher of the deaf in Mexico City, gained her Masters in Audiology in the US. Years later, she published an article in a Canadian audiologists' magazine bemoaning the fact that, "many audiologists in Mexico are *still* using non-selective procedures to select hearing aids.... Very few dealers have equipment to evaluate hearing aids in their offices and very few audiologists understand hearing aid specs."[16]

After completing her audiology degree, Regina Solomon had returned to Mexico in the 1980s and taught at universities and teacher training colleges instructing teachers how, "to do the job of the audiologist and hearing aid dealers."

And that is precisely what we needed to do at the Lakeside School for the Deaf.

Students' first hearing aids

From the very early days of the school, Paul Messenger, a retired American hearing aid dealer living in Ajijic, had donated his services to fit individual aids. These were provided by a hearing aid bank, established in Guadalajara in 1976, which collected used aids from the US for distribution to needy local children. However, Paul Messenger did not believe in the usefulness of hearing tests and audiograms; when selecting and fitting aids, he simply had the children indicate if they could hear a loud noise with the aid turned on. We felt that this was not necessarily providing students with the best available access to speech sounds. Fortunately, during classes, the children used the wired classroom amplification system, donated by the Indiana School for the Deaf, which amplified the teacher's voice better than their individual aids.

When Susan and I arrived, there were no student audiograms on file. Thankfully, there was an audiometer, so we immediately began testing the students' hearing. Then we needed to make two ear molds for each student before we could start using the more modern wireless FM systems with each group of students.

In 1983 we discovered that our students could be tested for free in Guadalajara by an audiologist in a government clinic. All Mexican audiologists are medical doctors with a one-year specialty in audiology. We felt a professional assessment of each child's hearing was important, especially for the parents' acceptance of the hearing loss, so we made an appointment for some students to attend the Guadalajara clinic. We watched as the audiologist sat in his office, with his feet on the desk, while his secretary did inadequate, very basic testing of the children in another room. He then signed the reports as the tester. Later visits, with other children, proved similarly unhelpful and resulted in at least one unfortunate misdiagnosis.

We had no better luck with the specialized testing of infants, toddlers and very young children in Guadalajara. For over a decade, I faxed the results of ABR (auditory brainstem response) testing by half a dozen private and government audiologists to Canada, for evaluation by pediatric audiologists. Their judgement was always the same: "Unacceptable procedures. Should not fit hearing aids on the basis of this flawed testing." Times have changed; today it is perfectly possible to get reliable ABR testing in Guadalajara, and excellent advice and service Lakeside from an audiologist in Ajijic.

Canadian International Hearing Services (CIHS)

The various services provided by the Toronto-based CIHS for over a decade, starting in 1985, were definitely a key factor in the Lakeside School's successful educational program. Thanks largely to CIHS, our classrooms were always equipped with (used) wireless FM amplification systems and our students wore individual (used/refurbished) good quality hearing aids when not in class.

Our requirements for mold-making materials, batteries and testing equipment were always met, and our staff learned educational audiology from Canadian audiologists in workshops sponsored by CIHS. Our classrooms could never boast the most modern audiological equipment found in Canadian and US schools for the deaf, nor the specialized monitoring by school-based pediatric audiologists, but the audiology services we provided at the Lakeside School were far ahead of what was on offer in schools and classes for the deaf in the state of Jalisco in the 1980s.

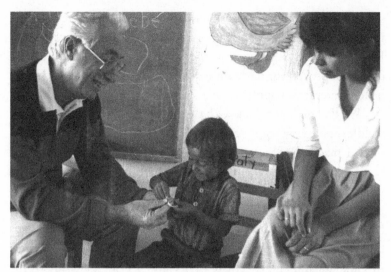

Gordon Kerr and Citlali show Mario how to operate his new hearing aid

Thanks to a continual supply of used aids from CIHS, we were able to fit free aids for hard-of-hearing students in local schools and some young adults from 1986 onwards. We also acted as a clearing house for all types of hearing and speech problems. We made appointments with various government specialists in Guadalajara and followed up on recommendations, including the fitting of hearing aids.

The first on-site visit by CIHS was in early 1985, when its executive director, Gordon Kerr, and secretary-treasurer, Alfred "Bud" Watson, met with Jackie and Roma and school staff. This was the first of many visits by Gordon and Bud. They both loved Mexico and enjoyed interacting with our students, advising on their hearing aids, helping with fittings and socializing with staff and Ajijic committee members, like Jane Osburn and Norine Rose, who provided accommodation in their beautiful Ajijic homes.

Gordon and Bud were both professors in the field of computer studies in Toronto, yet they managed to devote enormous amounts of time and energy to organizing CIHS activities, not only in Jocotepec and Guadalajara but in ten Caribbean nations as well.

Learning audiology

By October 1985, CIHS had made all the arrangements for our bilingual teacher Citlali Bravo and a Guadalajara DIF speech and language therapist to fly to Toronto for six weeks of training, with accommodation for both ladies at the home of Gordon and his wife, Doreen. The cost of the trip was covered by CIHS and a Toronto Rotary Club. Citlali spent part of her time observing teaching methods in total communication classrooms at the Toronto School for the Deaf and the rest of the time in the audiology department of Toronto's famous Sick Children's Hospital. The knowledge and skills Citlali brought back from Canada were invaluable in future years as she worked with new trainee teachers and helped with the never-ending tasks involved in ensuring that FM classroom systems functioned and that all students had working individual aids.

Citlali returned, not only enthused about the field of audiology, but with better mold-making materials. She immediately started making new molds for many students whilst I taught her math classes. For each student's FM unit we needed to make two personal, hard ear molds and then laboriously drill out a cavity to hold the metal button-receivers (speakers) in place. As younger students grew, their ear canals enlarged, causing squealing feedback and the need to make new molds every year or two for both the FM units and their personal aids.

Hearing aids in the 1980s were either "body aids" (small boxes worn at chest level) for young children, or large behind-the-ear analogue aids for older students and adults. The amplified sound could be adjusted, based on the audiogram, using a small screw driver to turn tiny internal controls affecting power output, treble and bass emphasis, and the compression of loud sounds. In those pre-digital days, such adjustments, and the assessment of outcomes, involved complex procedures and interactions and conflicting theorems.

So, in 1987, I jumped at the opportunity offered by Dr. Freeman King and his faculty at Lamar University in Texas, to attend summer courses in Practical Audiology. A Rotary scholarship was secured, enabling me to enrol in Masters level courses without paying out-of-state fees. Several staff generously provided free accommodation. The courses brought me up-to-date with the latest theories and procedures for selecting and adjusting hearing aids for children, and allowed me to practise more advanced hearing testing in a clinical setting. Armed with this knowledge, the Jocotepec staff and I continued to be responsible for the audiological services needed by our students.

In August 1989 Glen Sutherland, then head audiologist of the Canadian Hearing Services, Toronto, volunteered his time to conduct a full week of workshops, sponsored by CIHS, at the Lakeside School. Although officially school holiday time, all our staff and several teachers from Guadalajara attended each day. Glen's clear, well organized presentations covered relevant topics in pediatric and educational audiology. The CIHS newsletter of December reported that "Glen praised the work being done by Gwen, Citlali Bravo and the rest of the staff. Gwen reported that the seminars were very informative and well received."

In September 1992 Glen returned to Guadalajara for CIHS, training a local team to screen for hearing loss. He visited the Lakeside School again and conducted a two-day audiology workshop for the staff. Later, the CIHS newsletter reported that "Glen was very impressed by the teachers' understanding of audiology and their enthusiasm to learn more in this complex field." Glen was hosted by Phyllis and Georg Rauch in their hilltop Jocotepec home with its unrivalled views over Lake Chapala.

The following year, a US professor of audiology vacationing in Ajijic visited the school and agreed to hold a question and answer session with staff. He was surprised at the teachers' breadth of knowledge of educational audiology. After several hours of discussion, he stated that he just wished all the students in his audiology course (for future American teachers of the deaf) would achieve the level of understanding of these Mexican teachers.

Seeking hearing aids for students

From 1985 onwards, CIHS was our main but not sole supplier of donated audiology equipment, especially hearing aids, which they collected from clinics and other sources from across Canada. The Canadian hearing aid manufacturer Unitron was particularly helpful. With a growing student body, keeping our old, donated FM systems functioning in up to six classrooms was a very time-consuming task but was vital to the success of a Total Communication program. When the large, proprietary, rechargeable batteries in the student units inevitably died, they could not be replaced, so we needed more donated sets to keep all classrooms amplified.

Mildred Dovey, a retired teacher of the deaf and program administrator in Pittsburgh, sourced donated FM sets, hearing aids and educational materials through her professional contacts in Pennsylvania, returning to help teachers at the school during the tourist season each year from 1988 on. Supplies of hearing aids and batteries were also collected by many individuals, churches, service clubs and schools in Canada, the US and even Australia.

It was not all plain sailing. For example, in 1994 the Board misguidedly notified parents that there would be a fee of 100 New Pesos (a little over one week's minimum wage) for each of the new hearing aids donated by the Branscombe Family Trust and the Niagara Falls Rotary Club in Canada. After protests about the sale of donated equipment, this policy was cancelled and the money returned to the few families that had managed to pay.

Nearly all students were willing to wear their hearing aids consistently and thus became more aware of environmental and warning sounds. For profoundly deaf students, their aids helped them to hear a limited range of speech sounds and hence oral communication was often limited and a work-in-progress over a long period of time. For those with a less profound loss, a hearing aid could sometimes allow for rapid progress in spoken communication and

demonstrable changes in behaviour as we saw with Juan Carlos'
mother María, and with other students, including Teresa.

Teresa, from Ajijic, became moderately deaf at the age of 7.
Lacking a hearing aid, she never attended school until she enrolled
at the Lakeside School in her early 20s. She definitely lacked self-
confidence, spoke little and then haltingly, slowly and in a near
whisper. There was definitely "something wrong with her" opined
a family member. A year later, she was a smiling young lady who
spoke clearly and confidently even with strangers. Her family
could hardly find words to express their joy and excitement at the
changes in Teri. Her parents said, gratefully, "It's a new world for
Teri" thanks to the school providing a hearing aid and intensive
speech and language therapy together with literacy instruction.

I once fit a 20-month-old Jocotepec toddler, diagnosed with
a severe loss, with a body aid and two molds. A few weeks later,
her mother reported that the little girl liked her hearing aid and
indicated for it to be put on each morning. But, she had taken to
hitting the cat and annoying the baby till he cried, obviously curious about the yowls and shrieks she could evoke and now hear. She
had also started babbling when her mother talked to her.

Over the years, many tourists, snowbirds and foreign residents
carried donated aids and equipment from Canada and the US to
Lake Chapala for us. Miraculously, not once did we lose a single
aid at the border. The closest call must have happened to a retired
couple who were carrying in their van valuable sets of classroom
FM equipment and charging stations—a bulky cargo—and dozens
of donated hearing aids and cartons of batteries. A Mexican customs official told them to unload everything and began searching
their luggage. At the top of one of the first boxes he found a Bible.

"Ah", he exclaimed, "You Christian?"

Affirmative answer.

Now smiling and friendly, he helped pack their goods back in
the van and sent them on their way.

12

Funding and fund-raising

I marvelled at everything: Roma, Jackie, Gwen, Susan, members of the committee, the sponsors who, although not from my country, were so enthusiastic; their passion to help the most disadvantaged children was contagious. I was moved by these people who organized to help, to offer opportunities. And that was when I learned that in order to give, only the desire to do so is needed. There they were—María and Juan Carlos, Carmela and her mother, Juan Diego, Esther, Hermila, Mario, Juan and so many others—with their stories, their needs and their faith in these volunteers.
(Citlali Bravo, 2019. Citlali taught at the school 1984-1991)

The school and the expatriate community

When Jackie Hartley and Roma Jones stopped their camper van in Jocotepec in 1979, it was indeed a fortuitous choice of location for the school they would soon start. Eastward along the shore of Lake Chapala lay one of the largest North American expatriate communities in the world, centred on the towns of Ajijic and Chapala. It was members of that foreign community—full-time residents, part time snowbirds (winter visitors) and tourists—who would work together year after year to help guide the Lakeside School for the Deaf, to finance its growth and to participate in the life-changing education it offered to students. The school had support from the local Mexican community too, but its great advantage as a charity was its location beside a foreign population that included people with deep pockets and connections, people adept at organizing fund-raising events, and people who loved to help Mexican children.

The timing was also to the school's advantage. In the 1980s there were very few charities seeking financial help from the foreign and Mexican communities at Lakeshore. Most that did exist were providing scholarships to enable poor students to attend secondary school or university. Some of these were funded by local groups but some were mainly supported by out-of-country Christian organizations. By the mid-1990s, there was more competition arising, like the well-organized *Niños Incapacitados del Lago* which supported (and still supports) children with physical disabilities. Since the turn of the century, Lakeside has seen a plethora of charities, organizations and causes vying for attention, assistance and money.

Once installed in its permanent home in the converted chicken house, the school gradually become a focal point of the Lakeside area. Indeed, it was something of a tourist attraction, mentioned in best-selling Mexican guide books. This was largely due to our open door policy. Visitors, often the guests of full-time residents or winter snowbirds, were welcome any morning, no appointment necessary— the school having no telephone. This open access was unheard of in Mexican schools which often operated behind locked gates.

I was generally available to speak with visitors about the background of some of the children, about sign language, the teaching methods in various classes, the boarding program and the sometimes precarious funding situation. Visitors could then quietly watch class activities from the back of the classrooms, on the understanding that they would not be introduced and that staff and students would just continue with their lessons. Our visitors often remarked on the bright-eyed enthusiasm of the students at every level and the obvious dedication of the teachers.

As the school expanded, we offered a well-advertised, three-day Open House annually in the height of the tourist season. During the January 1987 Open House, over 100 visitors toured the school, many promising to seek help from home communities; we received donations totalling over $4,000.

First committee of the Lakeside School for the Deaf

Organized support for the school by the Lakeside community was in place by January 1982. A committee had formed the previous year with a membership list of some 60 individuals and Elmo Chatham as the first chairman. This committee, in consultation with Jackie and Roma, signed the rental contract for the 4000 square meters of land behind the house Jackie was renting. The chicken coop at the back of the property was a large, well-built shell divided into three sections.

The owner, Sra. Lola Urzúa, generously set the rent at only 1500 pesos (about $30 a month), with a three-year, renewable term. After several major devaluations of the peso, the rent was only about $5.00 by the end of the first three years.

With the committee now largely responsible for decisions affecting the growth and funding of the St Francis Lyn School, as it was then called, building renovations began in early 1982. Many members, both male and female, worked for weeks on the site. The earthen floor was cleared of weeds and a concrete floor was laid. Two volunteers strung electric wire from Jackie's rented house through the orchard to the school and then wired the building. The high interior walls were plastered and painted white, doors hung and plumbing for one bathroom was completed. One senior volunteer suffered from such a sore back and stiff neck after balancing atop ladders for days that he was unable to attend the dedication ceremony on March 21, 1982, when the school was renamed The Lakeside School for the Deaf.

The first AGM of the Lakeside School committee was held in January 1983 with 44 in attendance. The AGMs were always open to the public and there were no membership dues. Elmo Chatham was elected president of the Board of Directors. Further work on the building was reported with plans to buy kitchen appliances and install a septic tank and another bathroom. Two couples paid for a building contractor and two helpers to spend two weeks tiling the kitchen and installing kitchen sinks and appliances. There was also the need for part of the grounds to be levelled as a play area.

Soon after, construction began on a small bed-sitting room at the end of the building, intended for use by any volunteer teacher who might be enticed to Jocotepec by September 1982; however, with the snowbirds returning north, work slowed and only the walls were up when Susan and I arrived. The room would eventually be used as a small classroom and later became our resource and audiology room.

In 1983 the Lakeside School was legally registered as an *Asociación Civil*—a not-for-profit civic organization—under the name *Escuela Para Sordos de Jocotepec A.C.* As such, the Board of Directors needed to file an audited financial statement each year with a government department, and the school became eligible to apply for assistance from government agencies like DIF, the Family Development Agency.

The committee at work

The term "committee" was fairly loosely used by staff, parents, the Lakeside general public and the press to include: (a) the legally responsible Board of Directors (a minimum of five positions, usually many more) elected at each AGM; (b) the committee Chairs who volunteered to take charge of organizing specific events like the Rummage Sale, or tasks like publicity; and (c) the unofficial Friends of the School—supporters who helped with fund-raising events, assisted with special occasions at the school, provided transportation for excursions, solicited assistance from their home communities, became annual donors, or sponsored students.

Financially, the school depended on funding from three main sources: donations from individuals, periodic large grants (from foundations, international government organizations, and civic and church groups), and funds generated by organized social events at Lakeside. It was the "committee" in the broadest sense that initiated and fostered all three funding sources but it was the Board of Directors who decided on spending priorities and was legally responsible for the school.

Unfortunately, over the years there were few Board members who were comfortable speaking Spanish to non-English-speaking local authorities. As I explained in a letter to Susan van Gurp, "We need some bilingual Board members. Then I wouldn't have to be running around doing so much out-of-school administrative business, like meeting with the school accountant in Ajijic, and dealing with the authorities and tradespeople in Jocotepec."

School vehicles

Following my return to Jocotepec as school director in August 1985, I learned the Board was seeking a used car as an urgent priority, hopefully as a donation through an affiliate of DIF Jalisco. Without Roma to provide transportation, any needed contact with committee members cost me half a day at least in riding the hourly bus to and from Ajijic or beyond.

With no secretary and no telephone, all school business in Jocotepec involved teachers or me walking—after teaching all morning—to the Post Office, bank, stores, boarding houses, municipal offices, tradespeople, public telephone, local schools and so on.

I joked, in a letter to Susan in November 1985, that I'd worn a new pair of Birkenstocks to within a few millimetres of the cork—in only three months of cobblestone walking.

Once we had a vehicle, I knew I would need a Mexican driving license. Getting one involved bringing a photocopy of ID and proof of residence to the town traffic officer and paying 1800 pesos (about $6.00). There was no written test, no driving test, and I don't even recall being asked if I knew how to drive.

After three and a half months and endless red-tape, Ted Fisher, president of the Board, was told by his contact in DIF that the school would be allocated a 1969 VW Beetle. Ted discovered it had not been driven for over a year and was in such a sad state of repair that it had to be towed from the Guadalajara compound to the mechanic in Jocotepec in early 1986.

The Beetle was far too small for our needs, and mechanically quite unreliable, but at least I could drive to Ajijic. From mid-1988, when former student José M. was employed as maintenance man and chauffeur, he took charge of holding the old car together, used it to run errands for the school, and transported the littlest children daily to and from homes in the far corners of the town. Norine Rose then generously offered me the loan of a small car for my personal use as school director.

In March 1990 the committee newsletter reported the search was continuing for a used minivan, noting that used vehicles were expensive in Mexico and adding: "We could pay with gratitude but not much more." In response, Michael and Florence Weissman, long-time school supporters, donated a used Jeep Wagoneer that certainly helped the daily functioning of the school.

Unfortunately, that sturdy vehicle was written-off following a head-on highway collision in June 1992 when I was returning from school business in Guadalajara. No one was injured. The driver of the other vehicle was drunk and accepted full responsibility for the crash. Local authorities oversaw the payment of a large (for him) sum of pesos to the school as restitution, in lieu of being charged and fined. A small station wagon was purchased as replacement.

Fund-raising events at Lakeside

Obviously, without the tireless work of committee members from 1982 onwards, the school could not have survived and been able to offer life-changing education to so many students.

The 1983 AGM reported on local fund-raising efforts the previous year: four sold-out travelogue evenings and several recitals by concert pianist Rose Perry. A decade later, the number, variety and sophistication of fund-raising events for the school had ballooned. During the 1987–88 tourist season, fund-raising went into high gear for the "Save the School" campaign to help purchase the school property. Here are some of the events of that season, many of which already were, or would become, annual features on the Lakeside social calendar:

* The huge annual Rummage Sale in the Ajijic Plaza was initiated in November 1986. Organizers included Betty Matthews, Sydelle Schwartz and Georgette Richmond. There were no thrift stores at Lakeside back then, so there was great demand from the Mexican community for good used clothing, jewelry and household items. For the second annual Rummage Sale, a sell-out which netted about $1350, some students' families donated clothing and, at school, ex-students Martha (school cook) and Francisca (TA) prepared a huge quantity of candied pumpkin (*dulce de calabaza*), a popular, sticky, and delicious traditional sweet, for sale. The event, with the addition of a bake sale, morning coffee and Giant Raffle, was later renamed the Grand Bazaar.

* The first series of International Gourmet Dinners, in the 1987–88 season, was coordinated by Rubén Nuñez. Eight dinners, held in beautiful Lakeside homes, averaged 20 guests each at $25 a head, and were socially and financially highly successful. For each themed dinner, a different team of Friends of the School donated food and their gourmet cooking skills. Given the scarcity of gourmet restaurants in the area at the time, this popular but labour intensive method of fund-raising continued for years.

* House and Garden Tours were another hallmark of the committee's ambitious local fund-raising. Organized by Don and Eleonore Gould, these tours ran weekly though the snowbird season (November to April) from 1988 to 1994. Ticket holders could wander through five outstanding homes which differed each

Eleonore and Don Gould with four students prepare to entertain at the Gatsby Luncheon fund-raiser

week. Transport was arranged from downtown Ajijic and the La Nueva Posada hotel donated free drinks at the end of each tour. The generosity of the many home owners who opened their grand houses and gardens to the public was legendary. The program thrived because of the meticulous organization of the Goulds and their helpers in safeguarding the viewing properties.

* Cocktail parties, also held in luxury homes and tropical gardens, often with breathtaking sunset views over the lake, were always popular with locals, snowbirds and tourists, who enjoyed socializing with many others in otherwise inaccessible surroundings.

* The first Fashion Show was held in 1984. The sold-out event was repeated annually with equal success.

* A Dinner-Movie night in January 1988 screened the Oscar winning film "Children of a Lesser God," the moving story about a deaf woman and romantic love. This successful evening was repeated a few years later.

* Other imaginative, food-based social events included a riding exhibition followed by Sunday brunch, featuring horses

performing to Spanish classical music, a Spaghetti and Beer Bust, and a Dinner-Dance for Valentine's Day.

* Art shows and art auctions, with local artists displaying and donating works, reflected the long history of Ajijic as an artists' community.

* The Chili Cook-Off that began in 1978 was, and still is, an annual, heavily attended, weekend fund-raising event featuring music, entertainment, contests, produce booths and chili tasting. Proceeds were divided amongst various charities, including the Lakeside School. The committee's booth sold roast beef sandwiches some years and had brochures available for interested attendees.

During the 1989–90 winter snowbird season the committee was again hard at work at the Lakeside. All the many fund-raising events were again highly successful and all were complete sell-outs, such was the committee's reputation for organizing imaginative, high quality, fun-filled occasions.

The following winter (November 1990 to April 1991) was again a time of hectic fund-raising activity for committee and Friends of the School. Included in the schedule of events were the now standard activities of the Grand Bazaar, the weekly House and Garden Tours, the Chili Cook-Off, a Fashion Show and luncheon, a cocktail party for St Patrick's Day, and the Big Spaghetti Bash. The Gourmet Dinners, master-minded this season by Norine Rose, included two sold-out Chinese banquets for 35 guests each, gourmet Spanish, Greek and Italian evenings and a Sabbath dinner. In addition, there was a stylish Gatsby afternoon picnic while December offered a Louisiana Shrimp Boil, with fun for 100 guests, and a progressive Christmas Supper.

At some of these events, senior students from the school helped with food service, perhaps circulating with platters of hors d'oeuvres. At others, students provided entertainment with well-rehearsed folkloric dances, thanks to after-school-hours instruction by teacher Lupita. The colourful ribboned costumes were sewn by Eleonore Gould.

Beneficiaries

The major beneficiaries of all this creative planning and work were, of course, the students at the Lakeside School. Without the income generated locally by committee and Friends, we would have had to turn away deaf children who could benefit from the school's help.

However, the Lakeside community at large also benefitted from the frequent and varied fund-raising events. They provided local residents, tourists and the growing snowbird population with much appreciated social gatherings where they could dress-up and meet and mingle in some of Lakeside's grander residences whilst contributing to a worthy cause. Ajijic in the 1980s and 90s had no cinema, and few up-scale restaurants or classy cocktail lounges, so the Lakeside School committee's social events were much in demand.

One afternoon in Ajijic, an elderly lady knocked on the door of the house where a cocktail party for the school was due to start in a few hours' time. On finding that she could still purchase one of the last tickets to the event, she said delightedly to the hostess, "Oh, I'm *so* glad I can come. You see, my husband died two days ago, so I can come to your party." Later that evening she explained to the somewhat shocked hostess that her husband had been in a coma for many months before his death and that this cocktail party was her re-entry to Ajijic society. She even brought along her husband's hearing aids to be donated to the school.

For many of the hard working volunteers, the countless hours, weeks or months spent organizing events each year was their way of giving back to the Mexican community at Lakeside. Their contributions were visible, not only in the bricks and mortar at the school, but also in the changed lives of the Mexican children and young people. Some school supporters, like past-presidents Don and Eleonore Gould and Jean Carmichael, knew all the students and staff by name, and were given sign names by the children who always greeted them with big smiles and hugs. Beth Fisher also knew the children well enough to knit beautiful new sweaters for each of them in 1987.

Many friends of the school brought visiting family and friends to show off the pioneering school and the amazing teachers that they were supporting. In 1991 five members of the Daniels' family, who had established a trust fund for the school, celebrated the birthday of their mother, Norine Rose, with the students at the school.

Several snowbirds and expatriate residents have told me that the years they volunteered for the school were the very best years of their retirement.

Property maintenance by the students

The committee rented the school premises for almost seven years before purchasing the property. Until June 1985, Roma supervised the maintenance of building and grounds with the help of senior students and occasional assistance for some years from her part time gardener. Jackie financed the installation of horizontal steel bars across the open windows to burglar-proof the school in 1984. But, a few years later, some local children still managed to squirm in and rob the school of nearly all the sports equipment and a quantity of donated educational games. Vertical bars were then added.

When I returned to Jocotepec from Montreal for the start of the school year in September 1985, the school property was a mess. Roma was in Canada, recuperating; Jackie had moved and was renovating the old house where Susan and I had lived for two years. No one had cared for the school grounds through the summer rainy season. The weeds were chest high and vines were crawling over the roof and growing through the open windows (still lacking glass). Inside, two months' worth of dust covered everything. Jackie had, unfortunately, lost the keys to the school when she moved house during that traumatic summer, so I had to start by getting three padlocks sawn off. Teenager Mario from Ajijic, one of the original students from Lyn Hallinger's tutorial group, came back to school after working in house construction over the holidays, so we immediately employed him for an hour or so each day after class as gardener-maintenance man. He was assisted by three horses that did most of the lawn mowing for him.

In January 1986, 23-year-old José M. from nearby Zapotitán, profoundly deaf, illiterate, but capably operating his own small dairy business, joined the school (his first school) to learn to read. A few months later, César, almost 16, bright but also unable to read, enrolled as a boarding student, transferring from his village Junior High. These two took it upon themselves to work after school to organize whatever grounds and building maintenance needed doing. They didn't expect any pay; they understood that the school was paying for their education.

With José in charge, he, César, Juan, 19, and César's brother Miguel, 11, measured, bought lumber and constructed a lean-to carpentry workshop. The younger teens, accompanying José around town, were learning how to plan projects and comparison shop and how to deal successfully with storekeepers and trades-men, despite being deaf.

Together they later built a volleyball/badminton court on the grass, filling old tires with concrete to hold the posts for the net. The students also made several pieces of playground equipment for the younger children, using old tires and ropes, following designs created by Lakeside artist Georg Rauch.

When they were constructing a cow-proof front fence, I saw them cutting off branches from a big tree to use as fence posts. I got angry and protested. They all talked to me as if I was a 5-year-old with no sense. "That's the way to get fence posts in Mexico," they told me, insisting that, "In the rainy season, the tree will grow more branches." During the summer holidays in 1987, José and Juan painted the exterior walls white, with blue trimmed windows, and, with the help of a bricklayer, laid a concrete path from the front gate to the door. They also repaired and painted student chairs donated by the state social services. Eleonore Gould later made cushions for the metal seats to match the curtains she had made to beautify the classrooms.

In the summer of 1988, José, having learned to read basic Spanish and now able to communicate freely in sign language, accepted full-time employment as the school's maintenance man, gardener and chauffer. For several years, Jim Kaye was the committee member in charge of supervising maintenance and landscaping. He was frequently at the school consulting with José or leading the athletics practice for the Deaf School Olympics.

The school building had not originally been designed for human habitation and lacked any form of temperature control. In 1987 ceiling fans were added in the largest room; sliding glass windows were installed to combat the January chill and the dry season dust. When a tile roof was laid on top of the existing thin roof in 1988, the decrease in temperature inside was quite noticeable and much appreciated.

Gifts in kind

Over the years, hundreds of individuals and groups donated goods that helped make the school undoubtedly the best-equipped special education school in the state and beyond. From Toronto came a spirit duplicator (mimeograph machine) in 1985, but it must have had a bumpy ride south as six pieces were found floating around in the box, unattached. I spent three hours after classes reattaching bits but only the middle section of the wax stencil would ink. Then the local printer also kindly worked on it for ages, unsuccessfully. Finally Rev. Ralph Carmichael, with an engineering background, managed to get it functioning. At last we had a means of making copies on the premises and *Escúchame* (Listen to Me) was born—a weekly easy-to-read school news sheet for parents and students. In the early 1990s, the British Embassy in Mexico donated a new British-made photocopier which secretary Meche and the teachers put to good use, expanding the teaching materials available for classroom use.

Every year, valuable donated goods were brought by returning snowbirds and other visitors. In 1989 alone, our newsletters thanked donors for class sets of Spanish language readers, a video recorder, a new sewing machine, many boxes of educational games, teaching materials, sporting equipment and clothing for the students. If the donor was known, our students sent off their own thank-you notes for gifts received. That May, Dr. Freeman King returned with a car load of supplies collected from his university. Students and staff always received a much deserved boost in morale from his visits.

One year, amongst several boxes of donated goods from the US, a large pencil case was found that felt unusually heavy. Below several layers of partly-used pencils, we found a Smith & Wesson handgun. Bringing firearms into Mexico was definitely illegal. Staff found a safe home for the gun in return for a donation.

Publicity and kudos

The English and Spanish language press covering Lakeside news was always supportive and was invaluable in bringing school and committee needs and activities to public attention. The local press included the Lake Chapala section of the *Mexico City News*, the *Colony (Guadalajara) Reporter*, *El Ojo del Lago*, the *Chapala Riviera Guide* and Spanish language *La Ribera*. Reporters' articles in these publications were almost guaranteed to be factually accurate. Lakeside writers like Kate Karns, Ruth Netherton, Katie Ingram, Joyce Vath, Mary Prud'homme and Tony Burton personally attended events such as the Christmas concerts, the Deaf School Olympics in Guadalajara and Jocotepec, inaugurations of new buildings, excursions to the coast, and fund-raising events.

The first publicity brochure about the school was initiated by Board president Jean Carmichael in 1986. Marvin Carmack took the photos, and Bob Deschamps did the layout, and designed a new school letterhead. An updated brochure was produced six years later by Mary Prud'homme and her publicity committee.

That brochure featured kudos for the School from Dr. Roy Jones, Director of the National Center on Deafness at California State University, Northridge from 1962 to 1985. After visiting the school several times in 1991, he described it as,

> one of the most exciting and promising schools I have seen. It is pioneering a way of reaching rural deaf children who would otherwise be denied education. The director and staff are dedicated, energetic, enthusiastic and forward-looking. Through remarkable cooperative effort the school is enriching the lives of deaf students who are being prepared for productive and independent living in their respective communities. It is a model which could—and should—be replicated in other rural communities in Mexico.

A professionally-filmed promotional video, with narration by Phyllis Rauch and starring personable young Mario M., was completed in 1991 thanks to generous donations of time and energy by Javier and Citlali Morrett, owners of a video production company in Morelia, with the help of the University of Michoacán Video Department. Copies of the delightful 12-minute video, "The Best Gift of All," were made available to all friends of the school to show in their home communities when seeking donations.

Gordon Kerr, writing in the newsletter of the Canadian International Hearing Services, declared that "The school is truly an outstanding example of deaf education and continues to be visited by many North American educators. The staff is to be commended for their dedication to excellence in education."

The Canadian edition of *Reader's Digest* carried a six-page article in September 1993 entitled "The Legacy of Rogelio's Smile." It described the history of the unique school, the role of the expatriate retiree community, and shared stories of the students' success. Supporters viewed this as an international stamp of approval for the school.

13

Buying land and building classrooms

Purchasing the property

By 1987 the Board, with Jean Carmichael as president, was considering purchasing the property. Anticipated enrolment for the school year starting in September 1987 was 30 students with five teachers. However, we had only three actual classrooms. The need for more rooms was quite evident to all who visited the school. The Board was, understandably, unwilling to construct classrooms on leased land.

Sra. Lola Urzúa, the owner, was willing to sell the orchard but needed to consult with other family members who owned the large adjoining lot. The family decided to subdivide both properties in the New Year, put in new streets and sell little house lots. One of those streets would demolish our little end room and carve through the kitchen, unless the Board purchased Lola's entire orchard, which was about one-third more land than we'd been considering.

The school had "first option to buy" and Lola's asking price was a fair one, at the low end of its market value. The 4080-square-meter property would be large enough to accommodate any future expansion; the location was ideal in terms of the all-important question of bus transportation; the back street, now the school's front entrance, was quiet and safe, and the replacement cost of the existing building was estimated at $10,000.

On October 31, 1987, the Board voted to buy the property. The total cost was about US$30,000 to be paid in two instalments. Within six days, Jean Carmichael phoned to announce that the Episcopal Diocese of Albany, NY, would donate $15,000 towards the purchase. Reverend Ralph Carmichael, Jean Carmichael and George Stahler were those responsible for obtaining such a generous and pivotal gift from their diocese. Jean Carmichael, then in her second term as Board president, was a staunch and tireless supporter of the deaf children and their school.

March 15, 1988, was a Red Letter Day for the Lakeside School. The newly-elected Board president, Don Gould, signed the legal contract for the purchase of the property and handed over the initial cheque for $20,000.

During the previous six month campaign to "Save the School", support had been unbelievably generous, from individuals who dug deep into their pockets to institutions and governments who gave us such a huge boost. The committee had ramped up the local fund-raising events to a new level and I was kept busy writing press releases and funding requests.

Prior to the signing day, a land transaction headache emerged: the three legal documents involved all had three different measurements for the land. Thankfully, a Mexican *notario* (specialized lawyer) in Chapala donated his services to sort out the problem.

Before any classroom construction could begin, a permanent front fence along Privada González Ortega was needed to safeguard future building materials from theft. I requested that the municipality officially survey and mark our 135-meter front boundary line.

The unpaved street ended just before reaching our property which fronted onto an earthen footpath and cow pasture. So, along came an elderly town employee who held up a string with a stone tied to the end, with which he eye-balled a line of sight along the street and placed boundary markers for us. I don't recall having to paying any fee for this service.

View from the school gate, 1988: typical village homes

Building new classrooms

The reason for buying the land was to be able to build more classrooms as soon as possible. It was largely thanks to the Canadian Embassy in Mexico that construction could begin on a new building, designed by a young Mexican architect, Martha Enriquez, just eight months after the land was purchased. I wrote a detailed funding request and Lakeside resident Allan Rose successfully argued the case for Embassy assistance. Allan Rose was the Honorary Canadian Consul for Guadalajara and Lakeside, and his wife, Norine Rose, was then vice-president of our Board. Fortune was smiling on the school. In August 1988 the Canadian Embassy officially donated 56 million pesos (about Cnd$30,000), sufficient to cover the construction and furnishing of two of the three planned classrooms, plus two bathrooms. That same month, and eight months pregnant, I went shopping for classroom furnishings in Guadalajara because the donation was in pesos and it was feared there might be a major peso devaluation at the end of President Miguel de la Madrid's six year term in November 1988.

Gwen, TA Francisca and her students outside new rooms, 1990

Construction began in November 1988. Three senior students were employed afternoons and Saturday mornings, learning valuable skills and earning money towards their transportation costs for the year. In April 1989, we began using the new, spacious rooms, to the delight of staff and students. The bare, interior concrete-block walls were covered with an inexpensive bulletin board material to display instructional displays and show off the children's work.

That year, the Canadian Embassy was busy changing ambassadors, so the official inauguration by the new Ambassador, Mr. David Winfield, was scheduled for February 1990. After the ceremony, attended by many state level politicians, the local representative in the House of Deputies for Jalisco gave us a personal cheque for US$5000—the largest-ever individual donation and the first major one from a Mexican citizen.

Adding a basketball court, 1991

With a donation of over $1,500 in 1990, school volunteer Margaret Green and friends initiated a drive to construct a multi-purpose basketball court. The dream became reality when the Brown House Charitable Trust in England, which supported youth participation in sports, sent a $5,000 cheque for the project. The Canadian Embassy in Mexico also added a large contribution. Local architect Lorenzo Varela designed and supervised construction of the court and, as a member of the local Rotary Club, waived his fee. Mayor Miguel Ibarra arranged for free transportation of the tons of required materials that we purchased. Virtually all the basketball courts at Lakeside were badly buckled and cracked due to the shifting subsoil around the lake. Our court was excavated to such a huge depth, and built with such a heavy, rock retaining wall below ground level, that, 30 years later, it is still in perfect condition.

Other institutional donors

The purchase of the land and construction of the new classrooms would have been impossible without the two major donors who generously covered half to two-thirds of the cost of each venture. Thankfully, these were neither the first nor the last of the significant grants from institutions that kept the school thriving and growing.

Back in 1983, Susan van Gurp and I, with assistance from the Montreal YMCA, had obtained funding from two major foundations. The Public Welfare Foundation of Washington, DC donated $5000 towards the 1984 operating budget, and responded to my follow-up funding applications with cheques for another $5000 in 1987 and a final $10,000 grant towards the 1990 operating costs.

The second foundation was the Clifford E Lee Foundation of Alberta which initially contributed Cnd$3,000. Because it was a Canadian donor, and because of our link to the YMCA, Wiley Stafford at the Edmonton YMCA was able to double that money through Alberta AID, the province's agency for participation in global development work. Then CIDA (Canadian International Development Agency), a federal government agency, tripled that $6,000 so that the school received a total of Cnd$18,000 (US$14,800) in

Thank-you card created for YMCA by all staff and students, 1992

instalments between 1984 and 1986 for operating costs. I then updated our funding application, and the March 1988 committee AGM applauded the announcement of another Cnd$18,000 donation for operating costs from the same Canadian sources.

There were many other civic groups that made substantial donations over the years, usually for general operating costs but sometimes specified for a particular use, like the St Giles Kingsway Presbyterian Church, Islington, Ontario which donated Cnd$3500 to furnish and stock the school library in 1992.

Private donors

Scores of individual donors pledged annual gifts of $10 to $1000 or more, sometimes sacrificing a new purchase or a gift for themselves to fulfil the commitment, for not all were wealthy donors. A sturdy wheelbarrow for the school was one local couple's requested Christmas gift from their family in Ontario. One of Lakeside's most colourful personalities was Iona Kupiek, who loved to travel but instead lived frugally in her little house in Ajijic; she sponsored up to eight local Mexican students to high school and university, and signed over her monthly US Social Security cheque to the Lakeside School. She loved to meet the children and attended any special celebrations at the school, usually with a huge pink bow in her white hair—which the students used as her sign name. In the early 1990s there were about 250 donors on the mailing list, although not all were active every year.

In 1990 a major, unpublicized donation from the Daniels Family Foundation of Toronto (the family of Norine Rose) established a trust fund with US$40,000, the interest being available for operating costs.

Sponsorship program

The important sponsorship program began in early 1982 when Jackie's son Campbell returned to Canada, after one of his trips to Jocotepec, with photographs and Jackie's handwritten biography of each student. As with all such programs, sponsors received updates, photos and, if possible, greetings from their sponsor child. When the boarding program began in 1985, an annual donation of $250 came close to covering the costs associated with boarding each student since Mexico was still a cheap place to live. By 1990 the Board calculated that boarding costs and teachers' salaries had nearly doubled, and found it needed to seek two sponsors for each student.

Funding for new vocational programs and multi-purpose rooms

The October 1992 school newsletter carried a worrying prediction of greatly increased operating costs in future years, but also announced the exciting news of new vocational programs to start in November, thanks to Bishop Denis Croteau and the Catholic Diocese of Mackenzie, in the North West Territories, Canada. The Bishop visited the school in October accompanied by volunteer vocational teachers Marie Pruden and Wendee Hill and parishioners Henry and Darlene Young who would stay in Jocotepec to administer the project.

Under an agreement with the Board, they proposed to develop three new teaching programs at the school—a large organic vegetable garden; jewelry making and art classes; and carpentry classes, once a permanent carpentry workshop was built. (chapter 11) The cost of the new programs was covered by the Mackenzie Diocese, the Bishop drawing on $27,000 raised by his parishioners, and the school did not need to contribute any of its operating funds.

The Mackenzie Diocese Outreach Project had originally arranged to develop these programs for the 180 children in the Catholic children's home *Niños and Jovenes*. However, Padre Macias decided, after the team arrived, that he did not want the vocational programs after all. So, luckily for the Lakeside School, the project relocated to the school, where there was plenty of room for the vegetable garden and where enthusiastic students were keen to learn new skills.

Also announced in the October 1992 newsletter was the plan for a new building for vocational education—a no-frills construction with a small carpentry workshop, a secure store room, and a large multi-purpose room to provide space for daily dressmaking and craft classes, and which could also serve for jewelry, music and dance classes, parent sign classes and meetings, and a multitude of other activities. The local press reported that:

> The Lakeside School for the Deaf is pleased to announce that Arne Olsen, representing the Branscombe Family Foundation of Niagara Falls, Ontario, Canada has presented a cheque to the amount of $5,000 dollars, matching that recently given by Bishop Denis Croteau of the Diocese of Mackenzie, Canada, for the construction of a new vocational building. Local donors responded with the purchase of a "brick" at $10 dollars each.[17]

The new building was dedicated in April 1993 and was immediately in constant use for vocational programs and special groups.

Mexican contributions

The Mexican community was always supportive of the school, providing a variety of important contributions, both small and large. During its early years the school benefitted from free classroom space, free banking services, low rental fees for the orchard property and store discounts on materials. Bilingual Mexican, Sra. Amelia Cuevas, was a director on the very first committee in 1982, and was then elected to the Board at the first AGM.

The provision of free bus passes was a huge saving for the committee and students' families. If the families had had to pay, few would have been able to afford the daily or weekly cost. Year after year, Sr. Carlos Mendoza and Sr. Alfonso Diaz of Auto-Transportes de Chapala (Guadalajara–Chapala–Jocotepec bus line) very generously supplied free bus passes to our students; this benefitted 15 students a day in 1989. As the boarding program grew, Don Simón Cuevas and Sons of Omnibuses de la Ribera (Jocotepec–Guadalajara line) also generously gave bus passes to students traveling on that northern route, providing an enormous help to them and their families. Bus fares were very expensive relative to the minimum wage.

Successive Jocotepec mayors and municipal officials were always supportive. They not only attended the school's various inauguration ceremonies, but provided free services like the use of the theatre for Christmas concerts, preparation and use of the athletics facilities for the Olympics, and use of municipal trucks during construction of the basketball court.

Many Mexican professionals donated their time and expertise for particular projects like the design and supervision of the multipurpose court by a local architect, production of the school's publicity video by professionals from the neighbouring state, provision of work experience placements after school hours, classroom instruction in specialist subjects like electricity or mask-making. Free medical and dental check-ups and treatment were provided by dentist Dr. Carlos Cera and pediatrician Dr. Hector Meléndez of La Floresta from early 1992, and free legal services were provided by Mexican lawyers to resolve occasional problems. Lakeside business owners provided work experience, apprenticeships and then full-time employment for many of our senior students and former students, when they could, more easily, have given the openings to hearing youths.

The role of DIF Jalisco—The Family Development Agency

State government assistance came in several forms, at times erratically but always appreciated. Starting in 1984 there was a cash contribution of about US$50 a month from DIF Jalisco. A very important contribution from the same social services department was the monthly dry food ration that helped support the boarding program and the daily hot snack. From the mid-1980s on, the dry goods, available for pick up each month from the Guadalajara distribution centre, included several sacks of dried beans (*frijoles*), a 50-pound bag of dried skim milk, a sack of sugar, bottles of cooking oil and sometimes extras like cheese, salt or cinnamon sticks. (chapter 5)

Parent Assistance

In 1993 the first Parent Association was formed following a motivating talk at the school by the president of Jalisco's Association of Parents of Deaf Children. Parents aimed to offer support with some maintenance projects, with fund-raisers like their established Christmas raffle, and with a suggested contribution of 1 New Peso a day to the cost of the daily snack. Some families sent eggs, corn or other farm products whenever they could afford to, in lieu of cash.

14

School Board stumbles

Modernizing Mexican Education: Higher pay for teachers

In 1988, shortly before the end of his six-year term, Mexican President Miguel de la Madrid announced plans for a "revolution in education", with the first objective being improvement in the quality of education by "professionalizing the teaching service." There were plans to lengthen initial teacher training programs to four years from the previous two, and to substantially increase teachers' salaries, eventually setting the base teaching salary at four times the minimum wage. As a first step, the federal government announced a major pay raise for all teachers nationwide.

In 1989 the Lakeside School Board granted our teachers an equivalent raise, to a "lowly take-home pay of barely $200 a month," as Don Gould (Board president at the time) characterized the new salary. The Board had always aimed to maintain our teachers' salaries on a par with take-home pay of local primary school teachers in order to keep our specialized teachers at the school, (though they still lacked access to government social security and other benefits), to keep morale high and to attract quality teachers in the future, when needed.

On learning of the federal government's long term plans to improve education and the teaching profession, Don Gould wisely predicted that one day the school would need to become a partner with the special education department in order to continue to board and educate the deaf children of the region.

The Board that year (1989) was also covering one-third of the cost of construction of the new classrooms from committee coffers and warned they could be "in the red" by the end of the year, "unless friends responded generously." Support arrived, not only in the establishment of the large Daniels' Family Trust Fund, but in a major increase in donations from individuals and from Lakeside fund-raising events in each of the following three years.

Further pay raises for teachers were announced by the government in succeeding years. Hard work by our supporters ensured that fund-raising managed to keep pace with the school's ever-growing budget. For example, in 1991 the operating budget for the year had risen to slightly over US$70,000. Treasurer Nancy Price's report, presented at the January 1992 AGM by incoming treasurer Paul Wendt (husband of Board president Alice Wendt), recorded that donations had exceeded expenditures in 1991 by a little over $3,000.

However, in mid-1992, after the government again raised teachers' salaries significantly (around 40%) to reach the promised base salary level of four times the minimum wage, the school's financial outlook was a lot less promising.

Friends of the school immediately organized additional, local fund-raising events, held for the first time ever during the non-tourist (summer) season.

The October '92 newsletter acknowledged that:

> While this salary increase is a move in the right direction for education as a whole in Mexico, it does pose a major problem for Lakeside School supporters (and all private schools) since salaries and related taxes and compulsory medical insurance made up over 70% of our budget in 1991. To make matters worse, interest rates have fallen drastically over the past year (worldwide) and the monthly interest from our Trust Fund has been effectively halved.

Given this situation, the school obviously could not afford to expand staffing or enrolment and so we had to turn away several unschooled deaf teenagers who wished to enrol in September 1992.

A new curriculum and Grade 6 certificates

Prior to 1993, our staff had decided that the traditional decades-old Ministry of Education (SEP) curriculum was so inappropriate for our students that we had never applied for Grade 6 accreditation based on that curriculum. However, by 1993, SEP had announced a new special education curriculum that more closely aligned with the curriculum and methodology that we had implemented over the years and our teachers said they could work within its structures without detriment to the students.

With Board approval, parents were told in October 1993 that the school would be able to grant Grade 6 certificates to qualified senior students, based on their completion of a modified primary school curriculum, as was the case for students in the Guadalajara schools for the deaf.

Our parents and students were eager to have this certification as Grade 6 was still considered a worthy end-goal for education by many Mexicans at the time and it opened the door to more employment opportunities, to many non-academic vocational training programs, and to enrolment in the junior high school for the deaf in Guadalajara.

At the February 1994 AGM, I reported that staff were working on this certification. We didn't expect any problems as our staffing, equipment and buildings easily met all the requirements. There would be some extra paperwork to be filed annually. But, shortly after the AGM, the Board reversed their previous decision.

Staff and parent protests led to another reversal, with the Board finally agreeing that staff continue with preparation of the final documents. Then, as the deadline for filing approached, Board president Alice Wendt changed her mind yet again and refused

Prospective candidates for Grade 6 certificates sign to themselves as they read

to sign the document as the school's legal representative, saying they "needed to think about it... maybe next year." For our class of seniors, next year was too late: they would be leaving without their Grade 6 certificates.

This incensed many supporters. As Ralph Carmichael protested, "Next to the birth certificate, many Mexican parents consider the Grade 6 Certificate the most important document one can possess. Parents of our older students are up in arms over the Board's rejection of this opportunity."

I can only surmise that Alice Wendt and fellow Board members were determined to maintain complete control over "their" project without any input from Mexican educational authorities, regardless of the future welfare of the students.

Financial confusion

The October 1992 newsletter had asked donors, "How can we continue to provide the same level of services to students, present and future, who so need our help?" But, in the newsletters of April and December 1993, the Board (with Alice Wendt now in her second term as president) made no mention of any financial problems, or made any appeal for additional help, though they did supply the legal name of the Association, in case anyone wished to name the school as a beneficiary in their will.

The 1992 Treasurer's Report was presented, only orally, to the AGM in January 1993 by Paul Wendt. Viewing his spreadsheets later, I calculated that the salary expenditure had been overstated by many thousands of dollars due to an error in the addition of the salary figures, but I don't believe anyone on the Board seriously investigated this.

During 1992, with Paul Wendt as treasurer, there was no complete or reliable information available to the correspondence secretary regarding incoming donation amounts and donor names and addresses. Hearing that Paul Wendt intended to stand for a second term at the next AGM, I spoke privately with Norine Rose, an influential former Board president, explaining how confusing it was trying to work with our aging treasurer. Subsequently, his name did not appear on the Board's slate of nominations for 1993 Board positions.

In mid-1993 the Board, reacting to concerns from staff about their financial security, finally increased teacher salaries in line with the federal government's 1992 salary scale which completed the government's promise to professionalize teaching salaries. The 1993 total staff salary expenditure at $76,000 was approximately 52% higher than salary costs for 1991, with little change to staffing levels. Obviously, this posed a major on-going financial challenge to the Board and supporters.

Early in the New Year of 1994, the Board submitted a small funding request to the Alberta YMCA. It claimed a projected deficit of less than $7,000 for the fiscal year 93–94. However, only a few months later, at a public meeting of supporters in April 1994, the Board claimed in writing that there had been a net operating loss of $27,000 in 1993, following a net operating loss of $25,000 the previous year.

No audited statements were ever made available for either year, a lack of accountability that was noted in an open letter in March 1994 by Jean and Ralph Carmichael to the Board and the school's many supporters: "Neither the AGM in January 1993 nor the February 1994 AGM received adequate financial reports for the year."

This lack of accountability also led to the Canadian Group from Mackenzie Diocese ending their project with the school. At the end of 1994, the Group wrote that:

> In 1993 our project donated C$6,385 to La Escuela Para Sordos de Jocotepec, A.C. In addition, we provided volunteer skill trainers.... We were forced to withdraw our helpers from the school when the A.C. was unable to provide audited statements of income and expenses for 1993, which we needed to assure our donors in Canada that their money was being properly used.

Fund-raising: missed opportunities?

In 1992 the Edmonton YMCA, which had been helping the school financially for several years, paid for Board president Alice Wendt and me to attend a two-day Fund Raising Workshop in Canada. The workshop was excellent and stressed that the most effective fund-raising strategy was one person directly asking another person (or a group, like local doctors) for a donation.

Unfortunately, there is little evidence that Alice and the Board actually spearheaded any drive for donations based on this strategy. The following March, the Board started to organize a long term project to solicit donations from international corporations based in Guadalajara, such as IBM, Honda and Hewlett Packard. Six months later, they asked someone to help write a cover letter and had still not sent out any solicitation requests.

In another response to the financial crisis, two local residents (young foreigners) presented a detailed, written proposal to personally solicit contributions from the Mexican business community. On the basis of preliminary soundings, they felt quite optimistic. But Alice Wendt, in rejecting their proposal, replied, "The local Mexican residents are not receptive to helping any gringo efforts." Alice had been a Board member for six years, so must have known that many Mexican individuals and businesses had made significant contributions to the school ever since its inception.

During 1993, I had organized submissions seeking help from various international foundations. One of these, a German foundation, sent a representative from their Latin American office to visit the school and subsequently sent a package of forms to the Board for them to complete.

A similar project analysis package—addressed to me—was opened by Board treasurer Steve Penning in about May 1994. Because all the forms were in Spanish, the treasurer passed them on to someone else, but they were never completed or submitted. That German organization might well have been prepared to help. They were already funding 79 special education schools around the world.

The "State Option"

In December 1993 an ad hoc committee on Finances and Management, with some "outside professional members," was appointed by the Board to make recommendations for the 1994 fiscal year and future directions. The committee was led by Mr. Minor Halliday, who had never had any personal involvement with our small Mexican school; rather, he was a professional philanthropy consultant to multi-million-dollar Toronto civic organizations.

In January 1994 I was told by the new three-person Finances and Management committee that I had to submit a detailed 1994

Budget with a spending ceiling of $60,000. There was no collaborative discussion offered for a complex task involving decisions that were clearly not mine to make alone.

On January 31, 1994, I presented my response, finding that such a drastically reduced budget was not an acceptable option given the principles and priorities under which the school had always functioned, and given the impressive improvements in government special education services for the deaf in Jalisco under the "modernization process" of the past five years.

I reminded the Budget committee that special education for the deaf is a very expensive enterprise in developed countries and, as Mexican teachers' salaries were being "professionalized", the same was becoming true in Mexico. In Canada, the only private schools for the deaf have their teachers' salaries paid by the state and rely on fund-raising foundations to cover the cost of specialized services.

I compared what would be left of the Lakeside School's staffing on a $60,000 budget with the services now offered to deaf students in the three government schools for the deaf in Guadalajara and in the classes for the deaf in 14 of the new Special Education Centres now functioning in the rest of the state. Each Centre was assisted by a *Patronato* of professionals, local businesses, and civic groups, like Rotary, providing specialized equipment and services.

On a $60,000 operating budget, Lakeside School would have only 4.2 classroom teachers, no speech therapist, no teaching assistants, no secretary, no sewing/craft teacher and no cook. And, based on our current enrolment, Lakeside School would have a higher pupil-teacher ratio than the legal maximum in government schools, with none of the professional support staff —speech therapist, social worker, part-time Phys. Ed. teacher, teaching assistant, salaried vocational teachers and a school secretary—available to staff and students in those government schools. The facts and figures supporting my position were laid out in a four-page document presented to the Budget committee.

Given my findings, I recommended the Board consider two options:

1. Some reduction in staff and services, but only to the level where we still offered education close to, or equivalent to government centres. This would necessitate a huge fund-raising drive for sustainable funding of at least $87,000 annually thereafter.

2. Immediately investigate and begin negotiations with the State Education Ministry to integrate the school into the government special education system which would take over responsibility for staffing and salaries, whilst retaining the support of our strong community-based committee to ensure continuation and enhancement of vital services such as the boarding program, audiology and hearing aids, school vehicle, library, specialist teaching materials, excursions, bus passes and hot lunches. I suggested a two-year planning package with a budget of $87,000 for 1994, and a serious fund-raising drive while negotiations with the State were initiated and concluded.

On February 4, 1994, at the Finance committee's insistence, I wrote them a proposed 1994 budget at $87,000 with a month-by-month handwritten spreadsheet.

I was not given a copy of the 1993 Treasurer's Report prior to the 1994 AGM on February 15, at which the Board gave no hint that they were still considering a $60,000 budget for the year. In an extraordinary breach of their responsibilities to the membership, and to the school's staff and students, the Board failed to present any budget proposal for 1994, with the president simply stating that the budget would be substantially reduced in order to assure the continuance of the school. Long-term supporters, such as Jean and Ralph Carmichael, would later lament that, "The Board at the AGM in February 1994 gave no inkling of the drastic actions they had in mind and did not allow us (Friends of the School) to contribute ideas and help."

Then, as I was leaving the AGM, Alice Wendt handed me a letter from the Executive committee of the Board, which she alone had signed, informing me that "the school will be operated during fiscal 1994 with a budget not to exceed $60,000 " and that I was to "proceed immediately to implement the cost reductions proposed by the Finance and Management committee."

I was stunned. There had been no mention of a $60,000 spending limit at the meeting just ended. I had no idea what the Board had in mind under such a budget, as no one on the Board or the Finance committee had communicated to me their "proposed cost reductions" that I was now supposed to implement.

I was then instructed to draw up a month-by-month $60,000 budget, even though the Finance committee already knew, from my January presentation, the severity of the cuts this would entail. I wrote to the president on March 7, 1994, stating clearly that the $60,000 budget I was being forced to prepare "definitely does not bear my endorsement as the path along which the school should be heading." This budget which never had my approval, was later used to discredit me in public and in the press. The Board even falsely accusing me of wanting to phase out the boarding program—the very core of the school's services.

15

Trouble at the school

A letter from the Carmichaels to the Board and Supporters describes what happened three weeks after the 1994 AGM:

> Lakeside School for the Deaf came into being out of profound human compassion. It has maintained this spirit, as its capacity to meet the widespread need of deaf children has grown.
>
> This spirit was rudely violated in the abrupt dismissal of Gwen Chan Burton on Thursday 10 March.... She was required to enter an automobile at the school in which were seated the president and the treasurer; asked to sign a document (which she refused to do); required to surrender all her keys to the school and ordered not to trespass upon school property in the future except in the company of a Board member. She was denied access to her personal belongings. Subsequently the padlock on the gate was changed. Severance pay was denied. She had been given no advance notice that she might be fired... The letter of dismissal states that the paid position of director of the school has been eliminated, on grounds of 'the precarious financial situation.'

A week later, president Alice Wendt told me that I was not to contact her at her home or by phone. Any communication was to be through the Mexican Postal Service.

Hearing of my dismissal, Gordon Kerr, Executive Director of the Canadian International Hearing Services, who had been a frequent and involved visitor to the school over the past decade, wrote to a Board member saying: "Gwen created such a wonderful work environment for the teachers and students that she is going to be sadly missed." He had no way of foreseeing how completely that collegial, co-operative work environment would be destroyed over the next 12 months.

The afternoon after my morning dismissal, as soon as classes finished, staff arrived at my house, shocked and bemused. From them I learned that my main responsibilities as director had been redistributed amongst three teachers: teacher Linda was appointed education director; Gaby became administrator; and Lupita was put in charge of audiology and hearing aids. These responsibilities came on top of teaching their classes, and with no extra pay.

Two of the other teachers—Nena and Abi—were dismissed in the next few weeks, with five days' notice and no celebration of their years of dedicated service. The remaining four classroom teachers and the speech-language-integration teacher then had to reorganize classes. This resulted in 10 or 11 students per class, a pupil-teacher ratio higher than the maximum allowed in government classes for the deaf.

By the end of that school year, June 1994, teacher Linda announced she was no longer prepared to carry the extra responsibility of education director. The position had involved far more time and work than she had imagined, and she had a young family to care for after school hours.

On the final day of August 1994, teacher Lupita was informed that her employment was ended, effective immediately. This was one day before the beginning of the new 1994-95 school year. The decision had been made at an un-minuted meeting held (between regular scheduled Board meetings) by Alice Wendt and only two other members of the five-person Board—Steve Penning the new treasurer, and Margaret Drewry, the incoming secretary, neither of whom had been involved in school affairs previously. This is how the Board dismissed an outstanding special education teacher. The government education authorities, however, recognized Lupita's abilities and immediately employed her as the speech and language teacher at the newly opened Special Education Centre in Chapala. On that same day, the three-person "mini-Board" also dismissed the two teaching assistants, both former students. Later that week, Alice insisted that neither of these TAs—Francisca and Lourdes—was hearing impaired or a former student! And this, after six years on the Board as secretary or president.

A written statement by members of the Mackenzie Diocese Outreach Project, in January 1995, summed up my situation post-dismissal: "Immediately after Gwen Chan was fired, the Board began slandering her in the English-speaking Lakeside community, attempting to destroy her professional reputation." A year later, Robert Vázquez was still inventing and spreading completely false accusations about me, despite denials of each and every story by parents, former colleagues and former volunteers.

A new school director

When the new academic year began in September 1994, the school had no education director, teacher Linda having refused to continue in that role, and teacher Lupita was gone, along with her knowledge of the audiology and hearing aid program. The Executive Board announced that teacher Josefina would be the new director. She had originally come on staff as a part-time dress-making teacher, had trained as a classroom teacher by 1991, and was now teaching a class of 11 students. That appointment was a particularly unfortunate choice, as Josefina had been the staff member least committed to the students and the school in the past. She had, for example, in early 1993 requested two months unpaid leave in the middle of the school year to try out employment as a supervisor at a new garment factory in Jocotepec, a position that offered a higher salary. She was granted only three weeks leave, after which time she decided to return to the school.

Director Josefina's first act was to demand the school keys from all the staff on the grounds that she couldn't be responsible for security if they had sets of keys. Staff refused to hand over the keys so she changed the locks. Thereafter, things went from bad to worse. There was one crisis after another with a power struggle between Josefina and the other teachers. The Board accepted Josefina's fictitious version of each event. In October, American educational psychologist Carol Mardell offered to act, with an interpreter, as a conciliator. Alice declined her offer, saying everything was "fine".

In October 1994 the Board fired Meche, the young secretary, for "insubordination to the director", paid her severance pay and then looked for a replacement. Meche was more bilingual than anyone else left on staff, so had acted in the school as a translator between Board members and staff. She could communicate well in sign language, was popular with students and teachers and had been invaluable in multiple roles in the school.

By the end of November, Carol Mardell and Maxine Marion, a former school administrator, were tasked with assessing staff and Board relations. Their recommendations, among others, included: that at least one member of the next Executive Board be bilingual; that Josefina should attend private coaching sessions to change her policies and behaviour as director; and that the Board must be willing to change in some concrete ways, including listening directly to the teachers, not just to Josefina. "The staff needs to be treated as professionals, not household employees." Also, a secretary should be hired by the start of the year with desirable qualifications to include, if possible, "spoken English and sign language"—exactly what the Board had lost by firing Meche.

In 1994 the Board changed the *Acta Constitutiva* of the school (the legal document under which it operated as a civil association) and duly registered the changes in the Public Registry in Chapala, claiming the new document had been acclaimed by a November meeting at the school attended by 51% of the membership as required by law. This meeting was later proven to be completely fictitious. By inventing this meeting, the Board had acted without any respect for the laws of Mexico or the rights of the membership.

Unfortunately, too many students with too few years of schooling ended their formal education at the end of 1994, when the Board was clearly contemplating closing the school. In June 1993, the school had been serving 44–45 students; by early 1995, there were fewer than 17.

Despite the difficulties, in December 1994 some senior students, having been denied their opportunity to obtain a regular Grade 6 certificate, were able to successfully write the tests for the "Adult Grade 6 Certificate," designed for students aged 15 or older. Even then, the actual certificates did not arrive before the Christmas vacation and, following the school's closure, many students never ever received their certificates.

1995: No salaried staff

For whatever reasons, financial and otherwise, the Board decided to close the school as of January 1, 1995. Believing that classes resumed on the 9th, they intended to contact parents by letter in the first week of January. Director Josefina informed them at a meeting on the night of January 1 that the new term began the very next morning, so they then decided to close it, and dismiss all staff, at the end of the first week of January.

However, they were thwarted by the teachers, by then all ex-teachers, who offered to hold classes without pay for the rest of the school year for the students' sake. The Board had to pay legally-required severance pay to all dismissed staff, averaging four months' salary each. Staff hoped the school would be incorporated into the Special Education Department by the start of the next academic year in September 1995. The Board insisted that Josefina had to be part of the "volunteer" teaching team, which ended any hope of a coordinated, friendly, team approach, as in the pre-'94 years.

Two of the now unemployed teachers were immediately snapped up to staff newly-opened afternoon Special Education Centres: Linda in Ixtlahuacán de los Membrillos, and Elizabeth in El Salto. In the name of the Board, an American snowbird couple— Betty Vázquez, formerly the volunteer music teacher, and her bilingual husband, Robert—took charge of the school on a daily basis.

In late February, Betty and Robert Vázquez, in league with Josefina, invented a pretext to move a family of four children after school one day from their long-term boarding home (with the Canadian volunteers of the Mackenzie Diocese group), against the children's wishes and despite the written wishes of their parents that they remain with the Canadian team.

The frightened children were driven to a house in San Juan Cosalá and, for two days, neither the parents nor the Canadian boarding hosts knew where they were. A second letter from the parents, this one notarized and translated into English, was faxed to just elected Board president Norine Rose on February 23. Despite this, four days later the children were again told their new home would be in San Juan Cosalá.

The children ran away from school, refusing to go with anyone, and raced back to the Canadian team house, extremely upset. A local notary (a lawyer) advised that the three adults responsible— Betty and Robert Vázquez and teacher Josefina—could all be arraigned for child abduction, as could every member of the Board on whose behalf these individuals had claimed to be acting. The four students, at their parents' request, transferred to the new Special Education Centre in Chapala for the remainder of the school year, while continuing to live with the Canadian team.

Next, Betty Vázquez barred two of the volunteer teachers from entering the school. It was no coincidence that those teachers had protested the treatment of the four boarding students. Robert and Betty Vázquez then went around to parents' homes to announce that Betty Vázquez and the young former cook, Clara, would now teach the children, instead of the qualified teachers now barred from the school. Clara could sign but did not understand any English; Betty Vázquez could not communicate in sign language and had very limited Spanish.

The Board claimed, verbally, not to have authorized this change of staffing, but would not dissociate themselves from the Betty-Robert-Josefina triumvirate, and did not ask the teachers back into the school. Instead, on March 18, they again decided to close the school, this time from the start of the Easter break in April, "for lack of staff." The Vázquez couple, snowbirds with no legal right to work in Mexico, were to return to the States in April.

In the end, Josefina and teacher Gaby continued teaching at the school for the final months of the school year, with only 15 or 16 students attending.[18]

After Josefina lost the battle over the four boarders, those students' files and free bus passes mysteriously disappeared. Five former staff and the leader of the Mackenzie Diocese project, immediately wrote to the Board to complain that:

> Josefina has apparently taken students' Grade 6 certificates to her home. She denied a request to provide parents of a former student, who now attends the Special Education School in El Salto with teacher Elizabeth, with her Grade 6 certificate and papers. Certificates, audiograms and entire files belonging to other students, some of whom require them to complete transfers to other schools, are missing.

16

A new beginning, 1995

I first presented the basics of the "state option" on January 31, 1994, to the Finance committee. Then, I gave a very detailed explanation in April at a member-initiated public meeting (which the Board members refused to attend) and, yet again, in September '94 at a General Meeting called by the Board. At both public meetings, there was widespread support from members present to investigate state affiliation.

I felt it was vital that Board members and all supporters of the school realize that education for deaf children across Jalisco had improved enormously in the previous five years. I reported that:

> the new special education centres, 14 of which offer classes for the deaf, are staffed by young, recently trained, energetic teachers and administrators, with modern ideas and teaching methodology that's far ahead of what we still see in many primary school classrooms around Lakeside.... With the exception of the boarding facilities, the programs and services of which the Lakeside School has long been justifiably proud, are no longer unique to our school, but are being provided by State Special Education schools working hand-in-hand with associations of local patrons. The Lakeside School could become a model for state and community co-operation—both Mexicans and expatriates—to the benefit of present and future deaf children in the area.

At the 1994 August Board meeting, many newly invited "Members of the Board" were present. At the end of the agenda, under "Other Business", it was revealed under questioning that there was only $15,000 left in the bank.

Joan Frost of Jocotepec, a supporter since Jackie and Roma's time, then asked what had happened to the idea of a merger with the Education Department. No one spoke against it, Alice Wendt said nothing, and the meeting agreed that the formal request be sent to the authorities.

Two and a half weeks later, the document, which required the signature of the president as legal representative of the AC, had still not left Ajijic.

Readers of the *Colony Reporter* were informed that:

At the September 28, 1994 general meeting directors presented a break-even budget of $62,850 for the current school year September, 1994 to August, 1995.... President Wendt described the budget as "quite realistic" adding the financial future of the school was secure for "at least another two years." However, secretary Joan Frost said, "We have few financial reserves" and went on to say she favoured "looking into the state operation of the school as part of the special education system."[19]

In October 1994 the enlarged Board voted (13 'Yes' with 2 abstentions, Alice Wendt being one) to send a delegation to negotiate with the Education Department. The delegation was to be Joan Frost, Carol Mardell and me. Next day, Alice Wendt made a unilateral decision that I was not to be part of the delegation. The following day she announced there would be no delegation because her husband plays golf with someone high up in state politics and will ask him to speak with the education department chiefs.

Eventually, negotiations began with government authorities. Bilingual Board secretary Joan Frost led the negotiating team, devoting countless hours to attending appointments and helping prepare documentation. The *Colony Reporter*, after investigating, declared:

> Joan Frost worked hard behind the scenes to convince the old board to take the first steps towards rescue of the school and to keep negotiations moving forward. Norine Rose, seemingly reluctant at first to pursue government affiliation, is also a realist.... Once in the president's seat (Feb. 1995 AGM), she supported the negotiations fully. Joan Frost, Norine Rose, former school director Gwen Chan Burton, and Jesus Ochoa Mendoza, a member of the parents' association, deserve much of the credit for the rescue of the Lakeside School from oblivion.[20]

Affiliation with the State Special Education System

The *Colony Reporter* of April 22 1995 announced that "On April 18, 1995, a general meeting attended by 60 people unanimously approved a draft proposal to integrate the operation of the school into the government education system through the Jalisco Department of Special Education."

On April 28, 1995, the formal contract was signed by Board president Norine Rose, secretary Joan Frost, treasurer Stephen Penning and state officials. As of September 1, 1995, the Lakeside School A.C. (the non-profit Civil Association) would provide use of the land and buildings rent free, in a 33-year contract, while the state would be responsible for all maintenance and repair.

The education officials agreed in the contract to provide a minimum of two teachers specialized in education of the deaf and, furthermore, to provide education for students with language, learning and other educational problems.

For those students enrolled in the deaf education program, the Lakeside School A.C. promised to cover costs related to transport, boarding, food, audiology, hearing aids and routine medical care.

My verdict in hindsight

Had the Board sought state affiliation in early 1994, when the idea was initially presented as a viable solution to the financial crisis, the Board would have been negotiating for the staffing of a fully-operating school with 44 students and thus could have requested qualified teachers of the deaf for five classrooms plus support staff for September 1994. Because of the Board's decisions and actions, by the time negotiations were taking place in early 1995, there were only 15 or 16 students still attending and thus only two teachers of the deaf were allocated to the new Special Education Centre. Several dozen students in attendance in 1994 and countless future students thus lost their access to the specialized education they so needed and deserved.

September 1995: A new educational institution

The name selected for the new Special Education Centre (*Centro de Atención Múltiple*, CAM) was "Gallaudet", thus honouring the history of the Lakeside School as a pioneering school for the deaf in Jalisco. Thomas Gallaudet was the founder of the first North American school for the deaf, which began educating children using sign language in 1817. Today, Gallaudet University in Washington DC is the only university in North America devoted specifically to the education of the deaf.

All public signage for the Jocotepec school now bears the Gallaudet name and also "Lakeside School for the Deaf—Escuela Para Sordos de Jocotepec."

The new school opened with two classes for the deaf, a director and a social worker and soon added an educational psychologist and some specialist teachers for students with learning problems. A much reduced boarding program for deaf students continued, funded by the Lakeside School committee

Today, 40 years after the founding of the Lakeside School for the Deaf in 1979, its successor, CAM Gallaudet, provides education in nine classes for some 80 special education students, including some deaf students who cannot be integrated into regular schools. Some well-built classrooms have been added, but the old chicken coop is still in use as the administrative centre of the school. An active local committee continues to provide funding for a daily nutritious meal for all students, supports a hearing aid program for deaf and hard-of-hearing students in the Lake Chapala region, assists with educational services, and provides improvements to the school property like the purchase of new playground equipment.

Jackie Hartley and Roma Jones would doubtless be delighted that their "Mexican Kids" project, despite once teetering on the brink of disaster, lives on—a dream realized.

Milestones, 1979–1995

1979 Jackie Hartley and Roma Jones start teaching 2 students.

1980 First Mexican teacher hired; first fund-raising (Canada); 6 students.

1981 Chairman: Elmo Chatham. 7-9 students.
Local committee forms and rents chicken coop for the school.

1982 Chairman: Elmo Chatham. 9-10 students.
Official dedication of Lakeside School for the Deaf.
First specialist teachers (volunteers) arrive from Canada.

1983 President: Elmo Chatham. 11-13 students.
First major grants from international foundations.
School officially registered as Mexican non-profit.

1984 President: Jane Osburn. 16 students.
School switches from ASL to Mexican Sign Language.
Committee initiates annual fund-raising events.
First annual Christmas concert.

1985 President: Ted Fisher. 20 students (2 boarders).
Initial visit of Canadian International Hearing Services (CIHS).
Roma attacked; recovers in Canada, returns in December.
Board appoints Gwen Chan as school director.

1986 President: Jean Carmichael. 20 students (3 boarders).
Jackie and Roma return to Canada; first school brochure.
Consultant Dr. Freeman King provides professional development.

1987 President: Jean Carmichael, 2nd term. 27 students.
School land and buildings are put up for sale.
Board purchases the property.
Start of major "Save the School" fund-raising campaign.

1988 President: Don Gould. 29 students (11 boarders).
Students compete for first time in Jalisco Deaf School Olympics.
Three-day excursion for students and staff to Pacific coast.
Construction of three new classrooms and bathrooms.
Mexican President announces major increase to all teacher salaries.

1989 President: Don Gould, 2nd term. 35 students in 6 classes.
Board raises teachers' salaries in line with federal increase.

1990 President: Norine Rose. 40 students (22 boarders) in 6 classes.
Jeep Wagoneer donated.
School hires first secretary.

1991 President: Jane Osburn. 40 students (22 boarders) in 6 classes.
Multi-use basketball court construction and inauguration.
School hosts 2-day state-wide Deaf Students' Olympics in Jocotepec.

1992 President: Alice Wendt. 43 students (22 boarders).
Start of Mackenzie Catholic Diocese, Canada, vocational programs.
Another major government salary increase for all teachers.

1993 President: Alice Wendt, 2nd term. 44 students (22 boarders).
New vocational-multipurpose building constructed.
Canadian *Readers Digest* article about school.

1994 President: Alice Wendt, 3rd term. 33 students from September.
Director recommends affiliation with State special education dept.
Board dismisses director and two teachers without notice.
State affiliation favorably received at Special Members Meeting.
General Meeting votes to investigate affiliation.
Board votes in favor but president later refuses to sign document.

1995 President: Norine Rose. 15-16 students (January-June).
Board closes school, dismisses all teachers.
Teachers continue working without pay.
Negotiations begin with Jalisco State special education dept.
General Meeting unanimously approves State agreement.
Formal 33-year contract is signed.
Centro de Atención Múltiple (CAM) - Jocotepec Special Education
    Center is officially inaugurated in September 1995.

Notes and sources

1 John Lychek, *Mexico City News*, 1979.
2 *Mexico City News*, March 21, 1981.
3 Katie Ingram, *Mexico City News*, March 21, 1982.
4 BC Women's Mission, *Vancouver Sun*, 1982.
5 Katie Ingram, *Mexico City News*, March 29, 1982.
6 Association of Canadian Educators of the Hearing Impaired. April 1983.
7 School newsletter, July 1989.
8 School newsletter, December 1986.
9 *Chapala Riviera Guide*, April 1992.
10 P. Kaplan. 1996. *Pathways for exceptional children*.
11 R. Conrad. 1979. *The Deaf School Child*.
12 Kate Karns, *Mexico City News*, March 1989.
13 *Chapala Riviera Guide*, April 1991.
14 *Colony Reporter*, March 2, 1991.
15 *El Ojo del Lago*, January 1991.
16 *Focus*, December 1996.
17 *Colony Reporter*, March 20, 1993.
18 *El Occidental*, June 1995.
19 *Colony Reporter*, October 8, 1994.
20 *Colony Reporter*, April 29, 1995.

International press articles about the Lakeside School included:
> *Vancouver Sun*, Canada, 1982. "BC Women's Mission."
> *Globe and Mail*. Canada, April 25, 1983.
> *Halifax Herald*, January 1984.
> *Newsletters*, Canadian International Hearing Services, 1986–1994.
> *The Pittsburgh Press*, April 4, 1988.
> *The Indianapolis Star*, May 4, 1989.
> *The Horizon*, World Union of Catholic Women's Organizations. January 1993.
> *Readers Digest*, Canadian Edition, September 1993. "The Legacy of Rogelio's Smile."

Acknowledgments

This book was written in 2019 to mark the 40th anniversary of the founding of the Lakeside School for the Deaf in 1979. Former colleagues, some parents and former students, and my husband, Tony Burton, all felt that the history of this special project deserved to be remembered and recorded.

My thanks go first to my family—to Tony for his encouragement and for editing and publishing the book—and to our son, Trevor, for helping design and create the book cover.

Susan van Gurp, my teaching companion for the first two years in Jocotepec, deserves special thanks for saving all the letters I wrote to her describing events at the school for over a decade.

Thanks go to the former teachers at the Lakeside School who have waited patiently for this book and who have answered my queries and added missing information; particularly heartfelt thanks go to Citlali Bravo, Lupita Olmedo, Gaby Escamilla and Linda Reyes.

For their enthusiastic response and helpful suggestions after reading early drafts, my thanks to Jim Brown, Susan van Gurp, Gillian Seal-Jones and Freeman King.

Photographs included in the book come from various sources, including visitors to the school, the 1992 school brochure and my own collection.

Author

Gwen Chan Burton, born in Australia, taught in senior high schools in Melbourne before moving to Toronto, Canada, where she led the special education department in a secondary school for a decade.

Having grown up in contact with a profoundly deaf cousin, Gwen had always dreamed of teaching deaf children. In 1982 she gained a post graduate Diploma in Education of the Deaf and Hard of Hearing from the University of British Columbia.

Gwen's experiences at the Lakeside School for the Deaf in Jocotepec between 1982 and 1994, first as a teacher and then as school director, are described in this book.

From 1994 to 1997 she ran *Audífonos Para Alumnos* (Hearing Aids for Students), a volunteer program supported by Canadian International Hearing Services to fit donated hearing aids to hundreds of students in government schools and classes for the deaf throughout the state of Jalisco.

After Gwen and her family settled on Vancouver Island, BC, in 1997, she continued her interest in audiology and hearing aids, became provincially licensed and worked in private hearing clinics.

Now retired, she visits Jocotepec annually to fit modern, donated hearing aids for children and youth in the Lake Chapala region in partnership with the local committee which supports the CAM Gallaudet Special Education Centre.

All proceeds from this book will benefit this hearing aid program.

To contact the author: info@sombrerobooks.com

Also from this publisher

Geo-Mexico: the geography and dynamics of modern Mexico
Lake Chapala Through the Ages: an anthology of travelers' tales
If Walls Could Talk: Chapala's historic buildings and their former occupants
Mexican Kaleidoscope: myths, mysteries and mystique
Mexico by Motorcycle: An adventure story and guide
Western Mexico: a Traveler's Treasury
According to Soledad: Memories of a Mexican childhood
Dilemma, a novel

sombrerobooks.com
Sombrero Books, Box 4, Ladysmith B.C. V9G 1A1, Canada